Tradivox Catholic Catechism Index
Volume 1

TRADIVOX
CATHOLIC CATECHISM INDEX

VOLUME 1

Edmund Bonner
Laurence Vaux
Diego de Ledesma

Edited by
Aaron Seng

2019
TRADIVOX, INC.
SOUTH BEND, INDIANA

This book is an original derivative work comprised of newly typeset and reformatted editions of the following Catholic catechisms, once issued with ecclesiastical approval and now found in the public domain:

Bonner, Edmund. *An Honest Godlye Instruction.* London, 1556.

Vaux, Laurence. *A Catechisme or Christian Doctrine.* Louvain, 1583.

Ledesma, Diego. *The Christian Doctrine.* English Secret Press, 1597.

© 2019 by Tradivox, Inc.
ISBN: 978-0-578-58596-3

All rights reserved. This book or any portion thereof, however accessed, may not be reproduced, distributed, or transmitted in any form or by any means; including photocopying, recording, or other electronic or mechanical methods, without the prior written permission of the publisher.

Unless otherwise noted, all illustrations are in the public domain. Cover design by Tradivox, Inc.

Tradivox, Inc.
South Bend, Indiana
www.Tradivox.com

The Manner of Execution at Tyburn.

Dedicated with love and deepest respect
to all the English Martyrs and Confessors.

Ora pro nobis.

Contents

Acknowledgments
Series Editor's Preface

An Honest Godlye Instruction (Bonner, 1556) 19
Introduction
    1. The Our Father and Hail Mary 23
    2. The Creed and Various Prayers 24
    3. Commandments and Virtues 28
    4. Good Works and Beatitudes 29
    5. The Sacraments and Capital Sins 31

A Catechisme or Christian Doctrine (Vaux, 1583) 33
Printer to the Reader
Author to the Reader
  SECTION I: The Catechism
    1. Faith 41
    2. Hope 49
    3. Charity 55
    4. Sacraments 77
    5. Offices of Christian Justice 95

  SECTION II: Concerning Ceremonies
    6. Sacred Signs 103
    7. Order of Mass 113

  SECTION III: Certain Brief Notes
    8. Four Strong Reasons 121
    9. Growth in Virtue 123
    10. The Sign of the Cross 129

The Christian Doctrine (Ledesma, 1597) 133
    1. Faith 135
    2. Hope 140
    3. Charity 146
    4. Sacraments & Piety 150

About This Series 159

Acknowledgements

THE publication of this series is due primarily to the generosity of donors. The appearance of this first volume is especially indebted to the vision and support of Mr. and Mrs. Phil Seng. May God richly reward their commitment to handing on the Catholic Faith.

Series Editor's Preface

SOME are surprised to find that when a given Catholic is asked to "look something up in the catechism," he may well respond: "Which one?" The history of the Catholic Church across the last millennium is in fact filled with the publication of numerous catechisms, published in every major language on earth; and for centuries, these concise "guidebooks" to Catholic doctrine have served countless men and women seeking a clear and concise presentation of that Faith forever entrusted by Jesus Christ to his One, Holy, Catholic and Apostolic Church.

Taken together, the many catechisms issued with episcopal approval can offer a kind of "window" on to the universal ordinary magisterium - a glimpse of those truths which have been held and taught in the Church *everywhere, always, and by all*. For, as St. Paul reminds us, the tenets of this Faith do not change from age to age: "Jesus Christ yesterday and today and the same for ever. Be not led away with various and strange doctrines."[1]

The catechisms included in our *Tradivox Catholic Catechism Index* are selected for their orthodoxy and historical significance, in the interest of demonstrating to contemporary readers the remarkable continuity of Catholic doctrine across time and space. Long regarded as reliable summaries of Church teaching on matters of faith and morals, we are proud to reproduce these works of centuries past, composed and endorsed by countless priests, bishops, and popes devoted to "giving voice to Tradition."

In This Volume

In the interest of safeguarding the integrity of doctrine, the earliest Catholic catechisms were typically first published in Latin – benefitting from the fixed meaning of terms in the Church's mother tongue. Afterwards, the same were often translated into various local languages for distribution among the faithful and use in the apostolate. The present volume reproduces three such catechisms, one of which (Vaux's *A Catechisme of Christian Doctrine*) stands as somewhat exceptional in that it was first printed in the English vernacular. Each

---

[1] Heb 13:8-9

of the three appeared in the midst of one of the gravest trials in Church history: the Anglican schism.

The first is *An Honest Godlye Instruction,* authored and promulgated by Bishop Edmund Bonner in 1556. It finds a place among the many "penny catechisms," so called due to their smaller tract size and relatively low printing cost. The author was the reigning bishop of London at the time when King Henry VIII first formally separated himself from Catholic unity in 1534. Unlike the heroic bishop John Fisher who suffered martyrdom rather than consent to the schism, Bonner joined with every other bishop of his nation in taking the tragic Oath of Supremacy, forswearing papal authority and submitting to the English monarch as supreme head of the Church in England.

However, when the Catholic Queen Mary Tudor took the throne some years later (1553-58), England sought absolution from Rome and was restored to Catholic unity. It was during this period that Bonner appears to have retracted his error, being reinstated as the bishop of London to begin the laborious task of repairing his own failure and the years of damage done by the rapid influx of heretical doctrines that had followed upon the schism. Among his efforts was the publication of his little *Godlye Instruction,* enforced as the official rudimentary catechism in London and adopted elsewhere in the country. Issued in Latin and English, the vernacular content of the first edition is reproduced in this volume, and the bishop's earnestness toward the work of Catholic restoration in his diocese can be felt in his Introduction:

> …[S]eeing of late days, the youth of this realm hath been nouseled with ungodly catechisms and pernicious evil doctrine (which is to be feared they will not forget)… it is thought good seeing the elder age is provided for in necessary doctrine already set forth, that the said youth should also have some help herein.

Unfortunately having been widely vilified by Protestant contemporaries and in many subsequent "official histories" of the country, the true qualities of Edmund Bonner's character as a Catholic bishop may be beyond the reach of objective historical study. It is worth noting, however, that when the Anglican schism resumed under Queen Elizabeth I (1558-1603), Bonner refused to renew the Oath of Supremacy or carry out government orders for the suppression of Catholicism in his diocese; charges for which he was arrested, imprisoned, and finally died in the Marshalsea prison in 1569. Contemporary Catholic writers regard him and the other bishops imprisoned during this time as Confessors and Martyrs, and the walls of the English College of Rome bear the inscription of eleven such bishops among images of the martyrs.

The second catechism included in this volume is entitled *A Catechisme or Christian Doctrine*, composed by the learned and well-respected priest of Lancashire, Fr. Laurence Vaux. Educated at Oxford, Vaux was ordained in 1542 and served for some years as Warden of Manchester College – a position that placed him in harm's way during the years of renewed religious persecution under Queen Elizabeth. After escaping to Louvain, Vaux was incited to compose a new catechism in English, to serve chiefly for children and the unlearned. First published in 1567, his catechism met with great success and went into six further editions from Louvain, Antwerp, Douay, Rouen, and Liège. The 1583 edition is reproduced here, drawn from the Chetham Society reprint of 1885.

After returning to England to undertake further covert missionary work (including the dissemination of his catechism), Vaux was captured in the summer of 1580 and jailed in the Gatehouse Prison. During one of his many interrogations, he was asked a fateful question: "What relation are you to that Vaux who wrote a popish catechism in English?" Upon admitting his authorship, Vaux spent several subsequent years in prison of which little is now known. The common consensus regarding his earthly end is represented by the contemporary MS Chronicle of St. Martin, with an alternate spelling of the priest's surname:

> The venerable Father Laurence Vause, Martyr... shortly after his profession, discharged the office of sub-prior and went into England, where he was thrown into prison for the Catholic faith and was famished to death, and so gained the crown of martyrdom, 1585.

Given its direct significance with regard to Fr. Vaux's earthly end, the reading of his *Catechisme* becomes a particularly profound exercise.

The third catechetical work included in this volume is *The Christian Doctrine* by the Spanish Jesuit Fr. Diego de Ledesma. Having left his native Segovia for Rome in 1557, Ledesma entered the Society of Jesus just months after the death of the great Saint Ignatius of Loyola. His reputation as a practical catechist and first-rate teacher of theology grew rapidly (his *Modo per insegnar la Dottrina Christiana* remains a fascinating study of past educational methods), and he published a number of theological works while also serving as Prefect of Students at the Roman school.

First composed in 1573, Ledesma's little catechism was repeatedly translated for the numerous Jesuit missions throughout the world, even well after his death in 1575. Having been prescribed by the Catalonia bishops for official use in that region of his native Spain (1588), this catechism soon found its way across the ocean and into the hands of Fr. Henry Garnet, Jesuit Superior of England. Having recently established his own secret press for the publication of Catholic books (a serious crime under the now-entrenched Anglican penal laws), Garnet translated Ledesma's catechism into English for the first time, publishing it in 1597. His is the edition reproduced in this volume, with a few woodcuts added from the Italian edition of 1604. Nine years later, Garnet was arrested and executed in London.

Editorial Note

Our *Catholic Catechism Index* series generally retains only the doctrinal content of those catechisms it seeks to reproduce, as well as that front matter most essential to establishing the credibility of each work as an authentic expression of the Church's common doctrine, e.g., any episcopal endorsement, *nihil obstat*, or *imprimatur*. However, it should be noted that especially prior to the 18th century, a number of catechisms were so immediately and universally received as reliably orthodox texts (often simply by the reputation of the author or publisher), that they received no such "official" approval; or if they did, it was often years later and in subsequent editions. We therefore include both the original printing date in our Table of Contents, and further edition information in the Preface above.

Our primary goal has been to bring these historical texts back into publication in readable English copy. We have therefore made a number of edits not touching upon the content (e.g., new typesetting, more consistent textual divisions, updated formats and annotations) to allow for easier navigation and cross-reference throughout the series, rendering each volume a unique derivative work. Where any original notations are obscure, we reproduce them without alteration. We have likewise remedied a number of typographical errors and certain anachronistic spelling and grammatical practices of centuries past, to facilitate easier reading.

At the same time, in deepest respect for the age and subject matter of these works, we have been at pains to adhere as closely as possible to the original text: retaining archaisms such as "doth" and "hallowed," and avoiding any alterations that might affect the original content or authorial voice. We have restored original artwork wherever possible, and where the rare explanatory note has been deemed necessary, it is not made in the text itself, but only in a marginal note. In some cases, our editorial refusal to "modernize" the content of these classical works may require a higher degree of attention from today's reader, whom we trust will be richly rewarded by the effort.

Woodcut depicting an early method used in the production of Catholic catechisms, circa 1568.

We pray that our work continues to yield highly readable, faithful reproductions of these time-honored monuments to Catholic religious instruction: catechisms once penned, promulgated, and praised by bishops across the globe. May these texts that once served to guide and shape the faith and lives of millions now do so again; and may the scholars and saints once involved in their first publication now intercede for all who take them up anew. *Tolle lege!*

Sincerely in Christ,
Aaron Seng

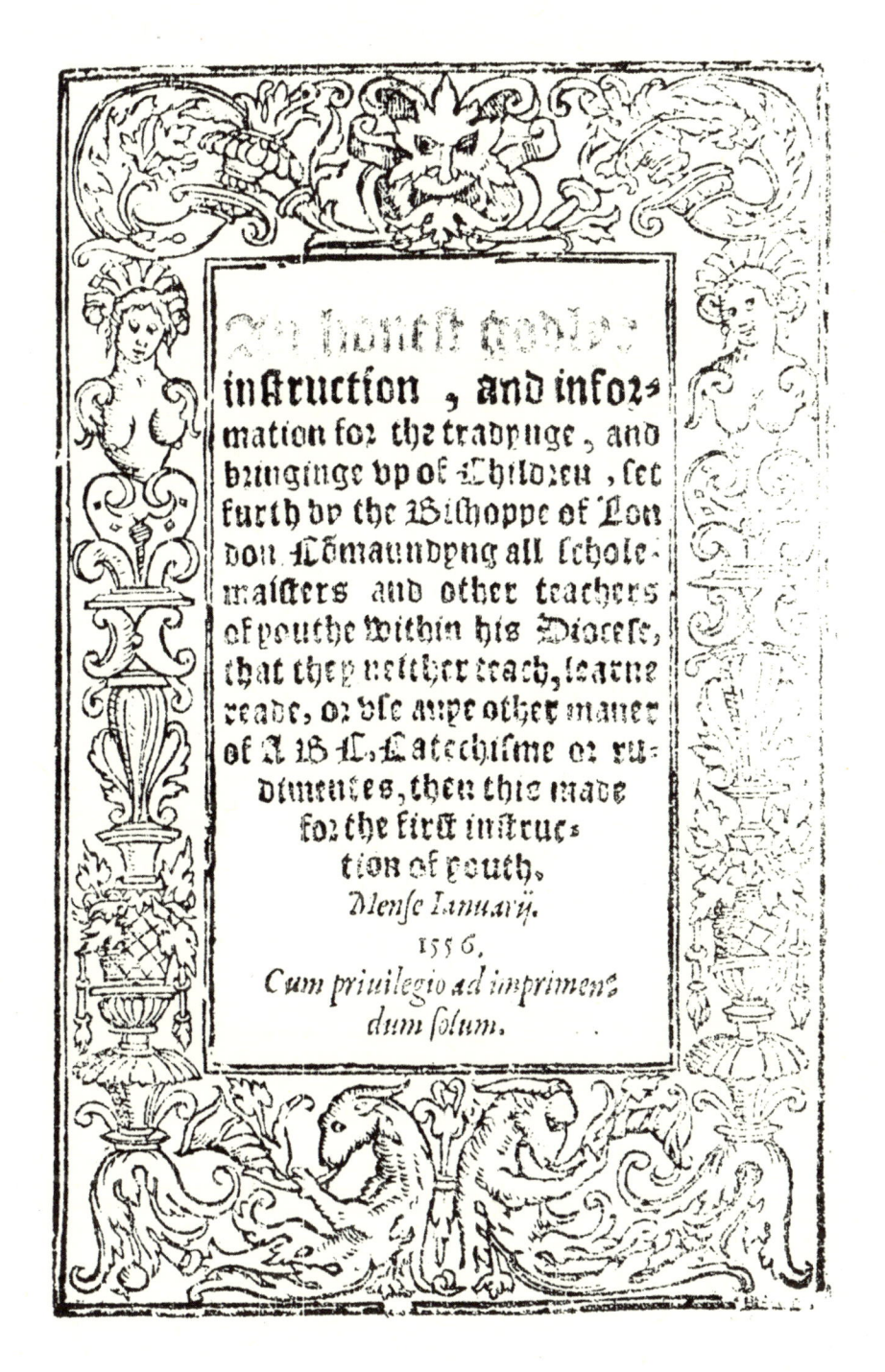

An honest godlye
instruction, and infor-
mation for the tradynge, and
bringinge vp of Children, set
furth by the Bishoppe of London. Cōmaundyng all scholemaisters and other teachers
of youthe within his Diocese,
that they neither teach, learne
reade, or vse anye other maner
of A B C, Catechisme or ru-
dimentes, then this made
for the first instruc-
tion of youth.

Mense Ianuarij.

1556.

Cum priuilegio ad imprimendum solum.

Original Title Page
(London, 1556)

An Honest Godlye Instruction
and Information for the Tradynge, and Bringinge Up of Children

Set Forth by the Bishoppe of London Comanndyng all Scholemaisters and other teachers of youthe within his Diocese, that they neither teach, learne, reade, or use anye other maner of ABC, Catechisme or rudiments, then this made for the first instruction of youth.

Mense January
1556
Cum priveligio ad imprimendum solum

Introduction

FORASMUCH as it is a meritorious deed to instruct youth in virtuous things, which youth of itself is propense and ready without any teacher to take and embrace vice, unthriftiness, and all manner of naughtiness, it is thought good (seeing of late days, the youth of this realm hath been nouseled with ungodly catechisms and pernicious evil doctrine, which is to be feared they will not forget, inasmuch as the new vessel long doth keep the scent or savor of the first liquor wherewith it was seasoned, according to the old proverb: *Quo semel est imbuta recens servabit odorem testa diu*; and that also the youth must have some honest introduction and entry in things convenient for them to learn – that is to say, both to know the letters, with joining of them together, and thereby the sooner made apt to go further both in reading and also in writing), it is thought good, I say, seeing the elder age is provided for in necessary doctrine already set forth, that the said youth should also have some help herein.

For which purpose, here briefly is set forth for them, as well letters of diverse sorts commonly used in this realm, as also syllables and joining of the said latters together. And as for words, sentences, and matters, such is here in this behalf also set forth; as is judged to be most necessary, apt, and requisite for the said youth to learn: As first to know how to bless themselves morning and evening; to say also the *Pater Noster*, the *Ave Maria*, the Creed, the *Confiteor* with the rest to answer the Priest at Mass; to say grace at dinner and supper; to say the *de profundis*; to know and learn upon the book and by heart the Ten Commandments of almighty God given in the old Law; the Two Commandments of God expressed in the Gospel; the seven principal virtues; the seven bodily works of mercy; the seven ghostly (or spiritual) works of mercy; the seven gifts of the Holy Ghost; the eight Beatitudes; the seven Sacraments; and to know by the book (and thereby to avoid) the Seven Deadly Sins.

All these things (jointly in Latin and in English, for the youth to learn thereby to read both the tongues) are set forth by the Bishop of London to be taught by all the schoolmasters unto the youth within his said Diocese of London; strictly charging and commanding all the said schoolmasters, and all manner of other persons within his said diocese, neither to teach, learn, read, or use any other manner of ABC catechism or rudiments than this, made for the first instruction of youth.

+ Bishop Edmund Bonner
London, 1555

Chapter 1

1. The Manner of Blessing

IN the Name of the Father, + and of the Son, + and of the Holy Ghost. + So be it.

Into thy hands O Lord I do commit my spirit; thou O Lord the God of truth hast redeemed me. So be it.

By this Sign of the Cross + let every wicked thing flee far away, and by the same sign, let everything that is good be saved.

By the Sign of the Holy Cross, + O Lord our God, deliver us from our enemies. So be it.

O Jesus of Nazareth, King of the Jews, Son of God, have mercy upon me. So be it.

2. Our Lord's Prayer

OUR Father, which art in heaven, hallowed be thy Name.
Thy kingdom come.
Thy will be done in earth, as it is in heaven.
Give us this day our daily bread.
And forgive us our trespasses, as we forgive them, that trespass against us.
And let us not be led into temptation.
But deliver us from evil. So be it.

3. The Salutation of the Angel

HAIL Mary full of grace, our Lord is with thee, blessed art thou amongst women, and blessed is the fruit of thy womb. So be it.

Chapter 2

4. The Creed, or the Articles of the Faith

I BELIEVE in God, the Father Almighty, maker of heaven and earth.
And in Jesus Christ his only Son, our Lord.
Which was conceived by the Holy Ghost, born of the Virgin Mary.
Suffered under Pontius Pilate, was crucified, dead, buried, and descended into hell.
The third day he rose again from death.
He ascended into heaven, and sitteth on the right hand of God, the Father Almighty.
From thence he shall come to judge the quick and the dead.
I believe in the Holy Ghost.
The holy Catholic Church.
The Communion of Saints. The forgiveness of sins.
The resurrection of the flesh.
And the life everlasting. So be it.

5. To Help the Priest at Mass

THE **Versicle**: And let us not be led into temptation.
The Answer: But deliver us from evil.
The Versicle: Confess to our Lord that he is good.
Answer: For his mercy is forever.

The *Confiteor*

I DO confess to God, to blessed Mary, to all the saints, and to you that I have sinned very greatly in thought, in speech, in omission, and in deeds by mine own fault. Therefore I pray holy Mary, all the Saints of God, and you, to pray for me.

The *Misereatur*

ALMIGHTY God have mercy upon you, and forgive you all your sins, deliver you from all evil, save and confirm you in goodness, and bring you to everlasting life. So be it.

> **The Versicle**: Our help is in the name of our Lord.
> **The Answer**: Who hath made heaven and earth.
> **The Versicle**: The name of our Lord be blessed.

The Answer: From henceforth, now, and for evermore.

Lord have mercy upon us (x3)
Christ have mercy upon us (x3)
Lord have mercy upon us (x3)

>**The Versicle**: Our Lord be with you.
>**The Answer**: And with thy spirit.
>**The Anthem**: The words following are of the holy Gospel of Matthew – Mark – Luke – John.
>**The Answer**: Glory be to Thee, O Lord.

Versicle: By all the worlds of worlds.
Answer: So be it.
Versicle: Our Lord be with you.
Answer: And with thy spirit.
Versicle: Lift up your hearts.
Answer: We so have, unto our Lord.
Versicle: Let us give thanks unto God our Lord.
Answer: It is worthy and right so to do.

>**Versicle**: The peace of our Lord be ever with you.
>**Answer**: And with thy spirit.
>**Versicle**: Go ye, the Mass is done.
>**Versicle**: Bless we our Lord.
>**Answer**: We give thanks to God.

6. Grace Before Dinner
THE Versicle: Blesse ye.
Answer: Our Lord doth bless.
Blessing: All that on the table are set or shall be, the right hand of God bless. In the Name of the Father, and of the Son, and of the Holy Ghost. So be it.

7. Grace After Dinner
THE Versicle: For such a feast let us bless our Lord.
The Answer: We give thanks to God.
The Anthem: Mother pray to thy Son, that after this exile, he will give joy unto us without end. So be it.

Versicle: After the birth of thy Child, thou didst remain a Virgin inviolate.

Answer. O Mother of God, pray for us.

> **Let us pray**: The Son of God the Father, for the merits and prayers of his godly Mother, bless us.
> **Answer**: So be it.

The souls of all the faithful being departed, by the mercy of God rest in peace. So be it.

8. Grace Before Supper
THE Versicle: Do you bless.
Answer. Our Lord bless.

Let him sanctify the supper Who giveth all things unto us. In the Name of the Father, + and of the Son, + and of the Holy Ghost. + So be it.

9. Grace After Supper
THE Versicle: Blessed be God in all his gifts.
Answer: And holy in all his works.

Versicle: Our help is in the Name of our Lord.
Answer: Which made heaven and earth.
Versicle: The Name of our Lord be blessed.
Answer: From this time now, and forever.
Let us pray: Vouchsafe, O Lord God, for thy holy Name's sake, to give to all doing good, everlasting life.
Answer: So be it.

> **Versicle**: Let us bless our Lord.
> **Answer**: Thanks unto God.
> **Anthem**: Mother pray thy Son, that after this exile he will give joy unto us without end. So be it.
> **Let us pray**: The Son of God the Father, for the merits and prayers of his godly Mother, bless us.
> **Answer**: So be it.

The souls of all the faithful being departed, by the mercy of God rest in peace. So be it.

10. The Manner of Praying for the Dead

FROM the deeps have I called unto thee, O Lord. Lord, hear thou my prayer. Let thine ears be attentive unto the voice of my prayer. If thou, O Lord, wilt narrowly look upon sins, O Lord, who may sustain it? But with thee there is mercy, and for thy Law have I abided in thee, O Lord. My soul hath abided in his word, my soul hath trusted in our Lord. From the morning watch until night, let Israel trust in our Lord. For with our Lord there is mercy, and plentiful redemption is with him. And he shall redeem Israel from all his iniquities.

> Lord have mercy upon us. Christ have mercy upon us. Lord have mercy upon us. Our Father, etc. Let us not be led, etc. But deliver us, etc.

Versicle: Grant to them O Lord eternal rest.
Answer: And let everlasting light shine upon them.

> **Versicle**: From the gate of hell.
> **Answer**: Lord deliver their souls.

Versicle: I believe to see the good things of our Lord.
Answer: In the land of the living.

> **Versicle**: Lord hear my prayer.
> **Answer**: And let my cry come unto thee.

Let us pray: Incline, O Lord, thine ear unto our prayers, in which we, being humble suiters, do desire thy mercy, that thou wilt set or place the souls of thy men and women servants (whom thou hast commanded to depart from this world) in the region of peace and light, and that thou wilt command them to be companions of thy saints, through our Lord Jesus Christ thy Son, who liveth and reigneth God with thee, in unity of the Holy Ghost, by all worlds of worlds. So be it.

The souls of all the faithful departed through the mercy of God rest in peace. So be it.

Chapter 3

11. The Ten Commandments of Almighty God
1. Thou shalt not have strange gods before me.
2. Thou shalt not make to thee any graven thing, nor any likeness of anything that is in heaven above or in earth beneath, nor of them that be in waters under the earth; thou shalt not adore them, nor honor them with godly honor.
3. Thou shalt not take the Name of thy Lord God in vain.
4. Remember that thou keep holy the Sabbath day.
5. Honor thy father and mother.
6. Thou shalt not kill.
7. Thou shalt not commit adultery.
8. Thou shalt not steal.
9. Thou shalt not bear false witness against thy neighbor.
10. Thou shalt not covet thy neighbor's house, nor desire thy neighbor's wife, nor his servants, nor his maid, nor his ox, nor his ass, nor anything that is his.

12. The Two Commandments of the Gospel
1. Thou shalt love thy Lord God with all thy heart, and in all thy soul, and in all thy mind.
2. Thou shalt love thy neighbor as thy self.

13. The Seven Principal or Highest Virtues
Three Divine or Theological Virtues:
> Faith, Hope, and Charity.

Four Cardinal Virtues:
> Justice, Prudence, Temperance, Fortitude (or strength).

Chapter 4

14. The Seven Works of Mercy Bodily
1. To give to eat unto the hungry.
2. To give drink unto the thirsty.
3. To receive into lodging or harbor the guests, or stranger that be needy.
4. To clothe the naked.
5. To visit the sick.
6. To visit and redeem the captives.
7. To bury the dead.

15. The Seven Works of Mercy Spiritual or Ghostly
1. To correct sinners.
2. To teach the ignorant.
3. To give good counsel to them that be doubting.
4. To pray for the health of thy neighbor.
5. To comfort the sorrowful.
6. To suffer injuries patiently.
7. To forgive offenders.

16. The Seven Gifts of the Holy Ghost
1. Fortitude or strength.
2. Counsel.
3. Science.
4. Fear of God.
5. Understanding.
6. Piety.
7. Wisdom.

17. The Beatitudes
1. Blessed be the poor in spirit: for theirs is the kingdom of heaven.
2. Blessed are the meek, for they shall possess the earth.
3. Blessed are they that do mourn, for they shall receive comfort.
4. Blessed are they who do hunger and thirst for justice, for they shall be filled.
5. Blessed are the merciful, for they shall obtain mercy.

6. Blessed are the pure in heart, for they shall see God.
7. Blessed are the peacemakers, for they shall be called the sons of God.
8. Blessed are they who do suffer persecution for justice sake, for theirs is the kingdom of heaven.

Chapter 5

18. The Seven Sacraments of the Catholic Church
   1. Baptism.
   2. Confirmation.
   3. Penance.
   4. Eucharist, or the Sacrament of the Altar.
   5. Order.
   6. Matrimony.
   7. Extreme Unction, or Last Anointing.

19. The Seven Deadly Sins
   1. Pride.
   2. Covetousness.
   3. Lechery.
   4. Envy.
   5. Gluttony.
   6. Ire, or Wrath.
   7. Sloth.

Imprinted at London, by Robert Caly, within the precinct of the late dissolved house of the grey friars now converted to an Hospital, called Christ's Hospital. The 28th day of November, 1555.

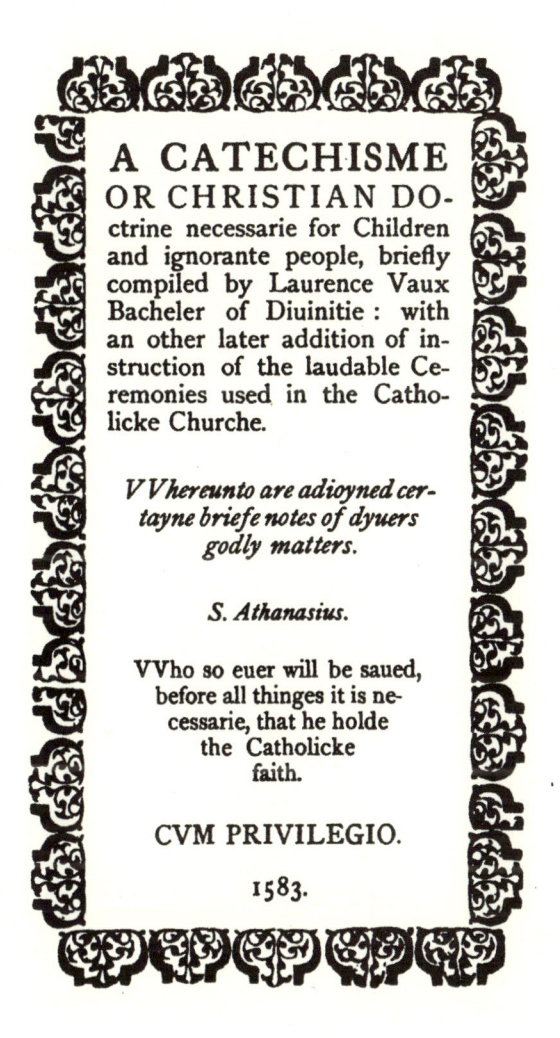

A CATECHISME OR CHRISTIAN DOctrine necessarie for Children and ignorante people, briefly compiled by Laurence Vaux Bacheler of Diuinitie: with an other later addition of instruction of the laudable Ceremonies used in the Catholicke Churche.

VVhereunto are adioyned certayne briefe notes of dyuers godly matters.

S. Athanasius.

VVho so euer will be saued, before all thinges it is necessarie, that he holde the Catholicke faith.

CVM PRIVILEGIO.

1583.

Original Title Page
(Louvain, 1583)

A Catechisme or Christian Doctrine
Necessarie for Children and Ignorante People

Briefly compiled by Laurence Vaux, Bachelor of Divinitie with an other later addition of instruction of the laudable Ceremonies used in the Catholicke Churche.

Whereunto are adjoined certayne briefe notes of dyvers godly matters.

S. Athanasius:

Who so ever will be saved, before all things it is necessarie, that he holde the Catholicke faith.

CUM PRIVILEGIO.

1583.

Printer to the Reader

OFTEN times I have heard many devout Christians complain of the scarcity and want of this Catechism, heretofore compiled and set forth by the reverend good Father L. Vaux; and have heard also many commend the same, as to be a book whereof they themselves and others have reaped much commodity.

Therefore I have long before this purposed to put forth this said Catechism; yet for that great volumes are written of the like argument in other languages, I deferred the matter, daily expecting some more ample discourse and such as might serve the turns of all, as well Learned as unlearned. But when I made some good men privy to this my purpose and expectation, it was answered that for an uncertain commodity to lose a certain—such a case were neither wisdom nor piety. For though it might be that some learned man would hereafter enlarge this argument and put it forth, yet it is uncertain when that will be; and when it cometh, it may perhaps not so aptly serve for young scholars and the unlearned (to whose use this short and compendious pamphlet was by the Author hereof first meant and pretended) as this does.

Whereupon to satisfy the desire of these good men, and to the intent and benefit of this my travail might grow to God's glory and to the furtherance and increasing of the Catholic Faith and Religion with the advancement of the godly intent of the first Author, I have to my charges and pains newly put forth in print this Catechism, with the instructions of the laudable Ceremonies lately added thereunto.

And finding in other godly books diverse brief notes of good and godly matters in foreign tongues not impertinent to this argument, I have thought good to collect, compile, translate and publish the same as an appendix to this book, for a further augmentation of profit and commodity to the unlearned; which travail of mine I desire may be accepted of all, as profitable to the readers as they may make it, and with as good a will as I offer it.

Author to the Reader

WHEN I did inwardly consider in my mind a Decree in the seventh Canon made at the Second General Council held at the Lateran, wherein Schoolmasters are straitly charged upon Sundays and Holydays to instruct and teach their scholars Christian doctrine appertaining to Religion and good manners (as the Articles of faith, the Commandments of God, and such like), and also to exhort and compel their scholars to be present in the Church with a reverent devotion in prayer (at the times of Mass, Matins, and Evensong) - the which Decree I did see diligently observed at Louvain and other places in Germany and Italy - these and such like considered, in mine own conscience I did confess a great negligence in myself, that I had not done my duty heretofore in bringing up my scholars.

Of these things upon a time I had talk with a grave godly man, who sometime did exercise an honorable room in England, and much pitied the lack of instruction of youth and the ignorance that was among the simple people there; and of a godly zeal that he had toward the salvation of the souls of the simple and unlearned, he earnestly requested me to set forth in writing an Instruction - what all people ought to believe and do, if they will be saved.

Whose request I was willing to satisfy for two causes: Partly to recompense my negligence, in that I had not done my duty in teaching and instructing them that were committed to my charge (taking comfort of the parable in the Gospel, that he which entered into the vineyard to labor at eleven o'clock received his penny equally with him that entered into the vineyard early in the morning to work – cf. Mt 20), and partly to join with the said godly man in the intent to do good to many and to hurt none; trusting that although I come late, yet this my simple Mite may be received with the poor widow's oblation (cf. Mk 12), although I was much afraid to have it put in print, lest it should come to the hands of such learned men as would look for finesse of sentence and eloquence of words (which are lacking in me), by means whereof in the end I feared, lest my good will and diligent labor should result in my rebuke and reproach.

Thus being in a great perplexity, it chanced that I had conference in this matter with a learned man, whose judgment I trusted better than mine own, and wholly depending upon his counsel I did forsake mine own fancy and will herein. And being animated and encouraged by my said learned friend to take the matter in hand, after my simple and rude manner, I have compiled this little book for young scholars and the unlearned; beseeching God in my daily prayers (if it be his will and pleasure) so to give his grace to the readers hereof, that some goodness may come thereby in the amendment of life, to God's to glory and their soul's health and comfort, which is the only purpose and intent that moved me to take pains to set forth this little book called *A Christian Doctrine*.

And what I have set forth in this little book, the ground and substance I have collected and translated out of the Scripture and General Councils, out of the books of Dr. Petrus de Soto, and Dr. Canisius, adding here and there some sentences of the ancient Fathers Sts. Cyprian, Athanasius, Ambrose, Jerome, Damascene, and Bernard. God send them ears to hear which shall learn it; and them that need not learn it because they know it, to take it quietly when they read it, knowing that I have made it for the simple and ignorant, and not for the fine fellows and learned.

To them of his Righte hande, come ye Ryghteous to lyfe euerlasting.

But to them of his lefte hand, goe ye wicked to hel fyre which is euerlasting.

Math. 25.

VVhen the Sonne of man shall come in his maiesty, and all his Angells with him, then shall he sit vppon the seate of his maiestie, and shall saye.

SECTION I

The Catechism

Chapter 1

1. What is man?

MAN is a reasonable creature of God, which God hath made marvelously of a body and a soul. As concerning the body, he is mortal like unto beasts. But as concerning the soul, he is immortal like unto Angels, made after the likeness and image of God; that is to say, with power of knowledge and love, apt to receive felicity and true blessedness, which consisteth in the clear knowledge and fruition of God.[2]

2. Whom do ye call a Christian Catholic man?

HIM that hath received the Sacrament of Baptism whereby he is made a member of the Catholic Church, and doth profess in heart, word, and deed the wholesome doctrine of Jesus Christ and of the Catholic Church, and doth not consent nor agree to any strange sects or opinions that the Catholic Church doth disavow or condemn.

3. How or by what means are ye made a Christian?

I AM made a Christian first by the special grace of God in me and his mercy; whereby (when I was the servant of the Devil and wrath) by Baptism he hath received me to be his child by adoption, when I could neither discern nor know it by my age. And also now by his special inspiration and grace (as firmly I believe), he hath persuaded this thing in my mind and made me certain that this Faith and doctrine of Religion, which I do hold and believe, he hath revealed in the Catholic Church, which hath been taught of Christ and his Apostles, and their successors to this day. And I am persuaded that same Faith and doctrine only to be true, and that it shall continue to the end of the world; but all other sects, false religions, and heresies which have risen from time to time, to be pernicious, hurtful and damnable.

4. Of what things ought a Christian man first to be instructed and taught?

OF Faith, Hope, and Charity, of the Sacraments, and offices of Christian righteousness. For although the doctrine of Christ and

---

[2] Gen 1

his Catholic Church be large and contain all the Holy Scripture with traditions unwritten (which we are bound firmly to believe), notwithstanding, under these five things especially all other things are contained and comprehended (either expressly in words or understood):

> 1. First, those things which appertain to Faith (that we are bound to believe) are contained under the Articles of our Creed.

> 2. Secondly, those things that appertain to Hope (and which we should desire and hope for) are contained under the petitions of our *Pater Noster*.

> 3. Thirdly, those things that appertain to Charity are comprehended under the Ten Commandments of God.

> 4. Fourthly, grace, mercy, and sanctification are given to us by the holy Sacraments.

> 5. Fifthly, by the offices of righteousness we are instructed and taught to decline from evil and to do good.

5. By what entrance must we come unto God?

FIRST we must come unto God by faith; for without faith it is impossible to please God.[3]

6. What is Faith?

FAITH is the gift of God and light whereby we be lightened within, and assuredly be induced to believe all things that be revealed in Christ's Church to us, either by word written, or unwritten.

---

[3] Heb 11

Of the Articles of the Faith

7. What is the Sum of Faith, or chief points that we must believe if we will be saved?

THE twelve Articles of our Creed that the Apostles made. Every one of the Apostles made one Article, as here followeth:

1. I believe in God the Father almighty, the creator of heaven and earth. (St. Petrus)

2. And in Jesus Christ, his only Son, our Lord. (St. Andreas)

3. Which was conceived by the Holy Ghost, born of the Virgin Mary. (St. Ioan Evangelist)

4. Suffered under Pontius Pilate, was crucified, dead and buried. (St. Iacobus Maior)

5. Descended into hell, and the third day he rose again from death. (St. Thomas)

6. He ascended into heaven, and sitteth on the right hand of God the Father almighty. (St. Iacobus Minor)

7. From thence he shall come to judge the quick and the dead. (St. Philippus)

8. I believe in the Holy Ghost. (St. Bartholomeus)

9. The holy Catholic Church, the Communion of Saints. (St. Mattheus)

10. The forgiveness of sins. (St. Simon)

11. The resurrection of the body. (St. Iudas Thaddeus)

12. The life everlasting. Amen. (St. Matthias)

8. What meaneth the first article? *I believe in God the Father almighty, Creator of heaven and earth.*

WE must believe in God the Father almighty, the First Person in Trinity, the Creator and Maker of heaven and earth; and of all creatures therein, both visible and invisible.[4]

---

[4] Gen 1

9. What meaneth the second article? *In Jesus Christ, his only Son, our Lord.*

WE must believe in Jesus Christ, the Second Person in Trinity, his only Son, our Lord; begotten of his Father before the beginning of the world, very God of the true God, light of light, being of the same substance with the Father.[5]

10. What meaneth the third Article of our Creed? *Which was conceived by the Holy Ghost.*

WE must believe that our Lord Jesus Christ was conceived in the womb of the Virgin Mary, taking flesh and blood of her (by the working of the Holy Ghost, without seed of man) which conception was immediately after the Salutation of the Angel Gabriel and her Consent. So he was born of the Blessed Virgin Mary after nine months, being very God and perfect man.[6]

11. What meaneth the fourth Article? *Suffered under Pontius Pilate, was crucified, dead and buried.*

WE must believe that Christ our Lord, being without spot of sin, was condemned to suffer death (Pontius Pilate being judge), was cruelly crucified, gave up the ghost upon the Cross, and was buried with great reverence of Joseph and Nicodemus.[7]

12. What meaneth the fifth Article? *He descended into hell, the third day he arose again.*

WE must believe that Christ's body lying in the grave, his soul descended into hell;[8] not to suffer pains, as some heretics do say, but for consolation and comfort of many Fathers there; and out of that place (called *Lymbus Patrum*) he loosed the souls of the blessed Fathers from captivity, and carried them away with him. The third day he rose again from death to life, manifestly showing himself to his Disciples, eating with them, and speaking of the kingdom of God.[9]

13. What meaneth the sixth Article? *He ascended into heaven.*

WE must believe that our Lord Jesus Christ, after he had done all things necessary for our redemption in his manhood, the

---

[5] Mt 16; Heb 1
[6] Lk 1
[7] Mt 20
[8] Mt 8; Lk 14; Eph 4; I Cor 15
[9] Acts 1

fortieth day after his glorious resurrection in the same manhood, marvelously ascended into heaven with great glory and triumph, carrying with him the souls which he had loosed from captivity and bondage of the Devil. And there he doth sit on the right hand of God the Father; that is to say, Christ ascended into heaven, is peaceably in great glory and majesty, and both judgeth and disposeth all things quietly and peaceably with God the Father in everlasting blessedness (which is understood by the right hand), where his seat was prepared from the beginning of the world.[10]

14. What meaneth the seventh Article? *From thence he shall come to judge the quick and the dead.*

WE must believe that Christ our Lord, at the day of judgment, in man's form like as he did ascend, so shall come from heaven to receive the good people to eternal joy, and to judge the bad people to perpetual pain.[11]

15. What meaneth the eighth Article? *I believe in the Holy Ghost.*

WE must believe in God the Holy Ghost, the Third Person in Trinity, proceeding from the Father and the Son, being equal in power with them; we must believe that he teacheth the Catholic Church all truth, and hath appointed the Bishops to govern and rule said Church, and that he sanctifieth us by the holy Sacraments.[12]

16. What is the meaning of the ninth Article? *The holy Catholic Church.*

WE must believe one, holy, Catholic and Apostolic Church; and we must believe the doctrine that is taught therein.

17. What is the Church?

THE Church is a visible company of people first gathered together of Christ and his disciples, continued unto this day in a perpetual succession in one Apostolic Faith; living under Christ the head, and under his Vicar on earth, our Pastor and chief Bishop.[13]

18. Why is the Church called one?

BECAUSE thereby are excluded all congregations of the malignant church which are divided into sundry schisms, sects, and opinions

---

[10] Acts 1; Mt 16; Lk 24; Heb 1
[11] Mt 25
[12] Jn 15; Acts 10
[13] Augustine, *Contra epistolam Manichaei*, Ch. 4

in doctrine; as the Lutherans' church doth not agree with the Zwinglians, nor the Zwinglians with the Anabaptists, etc. Therefore Christ's Church is called one, being gathered together in one spirit of Jesus Christ. In this Church is confessed and worshipped one God, one Faith is confessed and taught, one baptism and one uniform order of Sacraments are ministered without schism or division, having one Head in earth: God's Vicar in the Apostolic See, the successor to St. Peter.[14]

19. Why is that Church called holy?

BECAUSE in it we be sanctified and made holy in receiving so many benefits of God as we have received, the Church being Christ's dear spouse, the pillar and foundation of truth; Christ hath sanctified it by his precious bloodshedding; the blessed Martyrs have suffered cruel martyrdom therein; and many miracles have been wrought therein by the Apostles, Martyrs, Confessors and Virgins, for the confirmation of their doctrine.[15]

20. Why is the Church called Catholic?

BECAUSE everywhere, at all times, and in most persons, it both is and hath been.[16]

21. Why is the Church called Apostolic?

BECAUSE it is founded upon the Apostles, and in this Church we can show and prove by lineal descent in the See of Rome a succession of Bishops which have received and kept the Scriptures with the true exposition thereof; traditions and observations from the Apostles to these our days, from one to another, so that the true doctrine, principal traditions, general observations and customs used in the Church at this day, we are able to show instituted or allowed by the Bishops succeeding lineally to the Apostles Peter and Paul, which did sit at Rome, there laying a foundation of Christ's Church, and also suffered martyrdom there.

22. What is the Communion of Saints?

WE must believe that all good faithful Christian people – whether they be in heaven, earth, or purgatory – be members of Christ's Mystical Body (which is the Church) and communicate and participate

---

[14] Eph 4
[15] Eph 5; I Cor 6
[16] Mt 28

one with another. The Saints in heaven do pray for us in earth, and we participate in the benefit of their prayers and merits. We that be in this world do communicate one with another in prayers and the Sacrifice of the Mass, and with all good spiritual things that be done in the universal Church. We ought to pray for them that be in Purgatory, and they may participate with us in the Sacrifice of the Mass and in our prayers and other good deeds, and take relief and benefit thereof.

23. What meaneth the tenth Article? *Forgiveness of sins.*

WE must believe (if we remain still in the Catholic Church) to have remission and forgiveness of sins by the holy Sacraments that take their efficacy and strength of the merits of Christ's Passion.[17]

24. What meaneth the eleventh Article? *The resurrection of the body.*

WE must believe that although our bodies die and be eaten with worms or with wild beasts (or other ways consumed), yet at the day of judgment the same bodies with the same flesh and bones shall arise again, and be united to our souls again.[18]

25. What meaneth the twelfth Article? *The life everlasting.*

WE must believe that at the Day of Judgment, our souls and bodies shall be joined together; and we must come before Christ to give a reckoning of our own deeds. And they that have done well shall go to everlasting joy, both body and soul; and they that have done evil shall go to everlasting pains, both body and soul—so that after this life is an everlasting life, either in joy or pain.[19]

> *This is the Catholic Faith, the which except we wholly and steadfastly believe, without doubt we shall perish to everlasting damnation.*[20]

26. What is the sum of all the Articles of our Creed?

TO believe in heart and confess with mouth that our Lord God being most mighty in power, prudent in wisdom, of an infinite goodness, is one in nature and substance, and three in Persons: the Father, the Son, and the Holy Ghost; so that these Three are one true, eternal and incomprehensible God, of whom, by whom, and in whom

---

[17] Acts 1
[18] 1 Cor 15
[19] Mt 25
[20] Athanasian Creed

all things are.[21] Especially yet creation appertaineth to the Father, Redemption to the Son, and Sanctification to the Holy Ghost.

27. Who be alienated and utterly separated from the Church of Christ?

THE Jews, and all infidels, and they that by apostasy forsake their faith.[22] And heretics, which although they be christened yet obstinately defend error against the Catholic Faith.[23] Moreover schismatics, which separate themselves from peace and Catholic unity. Also they that be lawfully excommunicated. All these manner of people are excluded from the Communion of Saints, the participation of Sacraments, and the sufferages of the Church; which be clean void of a spiritual life, and are in bondage of the Devil.

28. What is the most plain rule of faith, whereby Catholics be discerned from heretics?

THE most plain rule to know a Catholic is: They that do profess the Faith of Christ and the whole authority of the Church, and steadfastly do hold the doctrine and Faith of the Church which the Doctors and Pastors of the Catholic Church do define and teach to be believed, are Catholics. For he that will not obey the Church (Christ himself sayeth), let him be taken as an Heathen and Publican.[24] He shall not have God to be his Father, who will not have the Church to be his mother.[25]

---

[21] 1 Jn 5; Rom 11
[22] Mt 18
[23] 1 Cor 5
[24] Mt 18
[25] Cyprian, *On the Unity of the Church*

Chapter 2

Spe salvati summus.
By hope we are saved.
(Rom 8)

29. What is hope?
HOPE is a virtue given from God above, whereby we look for the goodness of our salvation and everlasting life with a sure trust.

Of the *Pater Noster*

30. Whereof may we learn the right manner and way to trust and ask necessities of God?
OF our *Pater Noster*, which our Lord and master with his own mouth hath taught and appointed us to learn;[26] wherein be seven petitions, as here followeth:

1. Our Father which art in heaven, hallowed be thy name.
2. Thy Kingdom come.
3. Thy will be done in earth, as it is in heaven.
4. Give us this day our daily bread.
5. And forgive us our trespasses, as we forgive them that trespass against us.
6. And lead us not into temptation.
7. But deliver us from evil. Amen.

31. What meaneth the beginning of this prayer? *Our Father which art in heaven.*
IT IS a preface which putteth us in remembrance of an high and singular benefit that Christ our Savior hath obtained through his merits; whereby God the Father is content to receive and take us as his children and heirs by adoption. And by this sweet name of the Father, we are provoked and allured both to love him again, and also to pray with great trust.[27]

---

[26] Mt 6
[27] Rom 8; Gal 4; Eph I

32. What meaneth the first petition? *Thy name be hallowed.*

BY this petition we desire that like as God the Father is holy by nature, so by grace in the holy Sacraments we may be made holy and be sanctified; and that this gift of holy fear (lest we should offend God) be so firmly planted in our hearts, that thereby all corruption of sin be expelled and excluded from us; and that the love of God be so kindled in our hearts with pureness of life, that with all our might and strength we may endeavor ourselves to magnify, extol, and praise the honor, worship, and magnificence of the eternal Majesty; and whatsoever appertaineth to the glory of the most high and mighty God the Father.

33. What meaneth the second petition? *Thy Kingdom come.*

BY this petition we desire and ask the glory of the heavenly kingdom and everlasting felicity to be given to us, that speedily we may reign with Christ forever; which petition must be obtained by humility and meekness on our part, applying ourselves to God's mercy and pity.

34. What meaneth the third petition? *Thy will be done in earth, as it is in heaven.*

BY this petition we ask and desire the help of the divine grace to be given to us; that willingly, sincerely, and constantly we may fulfill the will of God the Father in earth, as the blessed company do in heaven.[28]

35. What meaneth the fourth petition? *Give us this day our daily bread.*

WE desire and ask that those things may be given to us which appertain to the nourishment and sustentation of the life of our bodies and souls, such as meat, drink, and clothing, the word of God, and the Sacraments of the Catholic Church.[29]

36. What meaneth the fifth petition? *Forgive us our trespasses, etc.*

WE desire pardon and forgiveness of our sins, being ready to forgive and remit what offense so ever any hath committed against us; and so he that is not with all men in Charity, can never truly say his *Pater Noster*. And as we show mercy, pity, and compassion upon

---

[28] Rom 8; Mt 25
[29] 1 Tim 6; Mt 4

the poor and to our inferiors that have need of us, so God will show mercy, pity, and compassion upon us.

37. What meaneth the sixth petition? *And lead us not into temptation.*

WE desire that in so great imbecility, frailty, and weakness of life, we may be underset and upholden with a divine power and strength; and that we may be defended against the Devil, the flesh, and the·world, lest by any means we be overcome with temptation of our said ghostly enemies, and give consent.

38. What meaneth the seventh petition? *Deliver us from evil.*

WE desire God the Father, that of all his gentile beneficialness he would deliver us from all adversities and miseries both of body and soul, and from all occasions of the same in this present life and in the life to come. Amen (which is as much to say in English as "so be it") signifieth the hope to obtain all that is contained in the petitions before going.

39. What is the sum of the four first petitions?
1. By the first petition we desire that the honor and glory of the Divine Majesty may be reverenced and hallowed among us.
2. By the second we desire our own felicity.
3. By the third petition we desire due obedience to God.
4. By the fourth, necessary sustentation of our bodies and souls.

40. What is the sum of the other three petitions?

THE other three petitions contain the evil things and miseries that we ought to put away with prayer: as sins, which shut up the Kingdom of Heaven from us; and temptations, which draw us from God to sin; and calamities both of this life and the life to come, except we be helped by a Divine grace. So our *Pater Noster* teacheth us both to ask good things, and to put away evil things by prayer.

Of the *Ave Maria*

41. Whereof came this manner of salutation to the Blessed Virgin Mary?

THE first part came of the example of the Angel Gabriel which with great reverence and humility did salute the Virgin Mary, being sent from God to show the wonderful Incarnation of our Savior Christ our Redeemer, saying: *Hail full of grace, our Lord is with thee.* The second of the example of St. Elizabeth, which being replenished with the Holy Ghost, did salute her saying: *Blessed art thou among women, and blessed is the fruit of thy womb.* Now the continuance of this manner of the salutation comes of the use and custom of the Catholic Church, being taught by the Holy Ghost this Angelical Salutation to be a very necessary prayer of laud and praise, to be often said, and to be joined to our *Pater Noster.*

42. What fruit or profit doth this Salutation bring us?

IT doth revive and stir up in us the gracious and healthful memory of the holy Virgin Mary and our Lord's Incarnation. And furthermore it doth admonish us and put us in remembrance that we may seek to get the gracious favor of the Virgin, to make intercession for us to God.

43. What may we believe of this Salutation?

THE excellent gifts and praises of the incomparable Virgin: that she was replenished and fulfilled with the gifts of God and the most singular virtues; that she was a Virgin and Mother; that she was blessed among all women of all times; that she was Mother of the King of all Kings, mother of Christ our Lord God. Also that she was the procurer of grace, and mother of life, which is Christ himself.

44. Why is the *Ave Maria* used so often to be said for a prayer, seeing there is no petition in it?

WHO so ever has any suit or request that he would gladly obtain of a Prince, Magistrate, or his Superior—he will use often words that will please and delight the mind of him that his suit is to, that thereby his mind may be moved with affection, and made attentive to hear the suiter and grant all his requests. So all Christian people are suiters to God, and ought to make suit and request for mercy, grace, and godly help to attain and come to eternal glory. And for because our Blessed Lady was preelected and chosen of God before all other creatures to be the Mother of Christ, both God and man, and of that glorious Virgin Christ took his manhood wherewith he redeemed us, therefore it is expedient to desire the said Mother of God to pray for us, that by her intercession we may the better obtain our suit of God.

No words can be found in the Holy Scripture of more efficacy and strength to move the Holy Trinity mercifully to hear our suit and grant our request, than the Angelical Salutation. First, what words can be more acceptable to God the Father than these words that he himself was the Author of, and (as one would say) "edited" in heaven, and sent them down into earth by his mighty Archangel Gabriel, when he had decreed man's redemption and salvation?

What words can be more pleasant to God the Son, the Second Person of the Trinity, than these words of the Angel whereby his blessed Incarnation is most specially remembered; that he being God was also made man perfectly, taking his Manhood of the most pure blood of the Blessed Virgin Mary, and was the blessed fruit of her womb; which fruit was offered upon the Cross for our redemption—the which fruit that the blessed Virgin brought forth is really present in the Blessed Sacrament of the Altar to feed and nourish the worthy receivers and to bring everlasting life to them that receive worthily, and also to be as a medicine to expel the poison of the fruit that Eve first tasted of, which brought death and condemnation to all mankind?

What words can more please God the Holy Ghost, the Third Person in Trinity, than these words that the Angel spoke to the Blessed Virgin Mary, by the which he did work the miraculous Incarnation of our Savior in the Virgin's womb?

So the will of the Holy Trinity was wrought by the Salutation of the Angel, to the great joy of Angels and to the unspeakable comfort of mankind. What words can be more joyful to the Blessed Virgin Mary than to hear these words that the Angel saluted her with, at the conception of our Savior Christ in her womb; when Eva was turned into Ave, declaring her to be innocent, without spot of sin, so full of grace as never any earthly creature was; in such sort and manner to have our Lord God with her as never any creature had; to have such blessedness as never any woman had?

Being a pure Virgin and Mother, without grief or pain, bringing forth such fruit of her womb as by his glorious Passion did redeem the world—what can more move the Blessed Virgin to pray to God for us, than the Angelical salutation (called commonly the *Ave Maria*), in the which is contained such mystical words (sayeth St. Bernard) that as often as it is said with a reverent devotion, it maketh angels glad and the devils to quake and tremble? Therefore upon these considerations the holy Church doth universally and daily use both in public and private prayer, this Angelical Salutation, and commendeth the same to all her obedient Children.

Chapter 3

Si vis ad vitā ingredi, serus mandata.
If thou wilt enter into life, keep the Commandments.
(Mt 19)

45. What is Charity?

CHARITY is a virtue given from God, by the keeping whereof (as Christ said) we shall possess everlasting life in the kingdom of heaven.[30]

46. How many Commandments of God be there?

TEN, whereof the first Commandment is: Thou shalt have none other gods but one: God the Father, God the Son, and God the Holy Ghost—Three Persons, and One God. Thou shalt worship thy Lord God and only serve him.[31]

47. What meaneth this Commandment?

IT doth prohibit and condemn all idolatry and worshipping of false gods, art magik, divination, superstitious observations, and all wicked worshipping. And upon the contrary part it requireth that we believe in God and worship him.[32]

48. How many manner of honors and worship be there?

THREE, which be called *Latria*, *Hyperdulia*, and *Dulia*.

49. What is the honor and worship called *Latria*?

LATRIA is a Service, Adoration, honor and worship that must be given only to God, being the beginning and end of every creature. By this honor and worship called *Latria* we must honor, worship and reverence the Blessed Trinity and Christ Incarnate, the Second Person in Trinity.

50. What is the honor, worship, and reverence called *Hyperdulia*?

HYPERDULIA is a reverence, worship, and honor due unto no other but to such as be most joined unto God: as our most

---

[30] Mt 22; Lk 10; Mt 19
[31] Ex 20; Mt 4
[32] Ex 23; Deut 18

Blessed Lady Mother of God, of whom Christ took his manhood.

51. What is the honor, worship, and reverence, that is called *Dulia*?

DULIA is a reverence, worship, and honor appertaining to reverend persons both in heaven and in earth. By this honor called *Dulia* we worship and honor the Angels and Saints in heaven. But we do not honor and worship Saints as putting more confidence and trust in them than in God, nor with such honor as is due to God. For we honor them as the friends of God, being his Children and heirs by grace, and our Advocates and Intercessors with God the Giver of all honor. In earth we reverence their Relics and Images, but the honor is referred to the Saints themselves. Also with this honor of *Dulia* we honor our Parents, Superiors, and all reverend persons.[33]

52. How is God's due honor and service given him?

IN our hearts by faith, hope, and charity. In our bodies by outward gesture and acts, as Sacrifice and fasting, etc.

53. How is it given by Faith?

IN believing the Twelve Articles of our Creed, both expressed in words and understood as holy Church doth believe and teach; and in having an inward devotion of mind toward God, and his Saints for his sake.

54. How must we honor God by Hope?

WE must have a steadfast trust in God, that of his mercy and grace (our good works answering thereunto) he will reward us with everlasting joy in heaven.

55. How must we honor God by Charity?

WE must love God with all our hearts, so firmly that neither for fear nor flattery, prosperity, nor adversity we be carried away from God.[34] And that the love of no creature remain in our hearts, but for God and godliness. With all our souls we must love God so faithfully that we had rather our souls should be severed from our bodies than from God. This love maketh all things light and easy; this love caused the glorious Martyrs to suffer all kind of torments both patiently and gladly for the fervent love of God. This ardent love unto

---

[33] John Damascene, *De fide orthodoxa*, Bk. 4, Ch. 16
[34] Mt 22

God caused the blessed Fathers in wilderness to take great pains and penance upon them, in fasting and praying, weeping and mourning. For their meat and drink they used dry bread and cold water, herbs, roots, and bark of trees; for their clothing, hair and sack; the cold earth for a bed; a hard stone for a pillow; and were ready to suffer any cruel death for Christ's sake, their hearts were so kindled with a burning Charity towards God.

56. How many ways is the First Commandment broken concerning Faith?

SEVEN manner of ways, that is to say:
1. By Infidelity
2. Doubting in faith
3. Presumptuous searching of faith
4. Denying of faith
5. Tempting of God
6. Unreverence of God
7. The Art Magik*

57. Who be they that break the First Commandment of God by Infidelity?

ALL heretics, idolaters, Turks and Jews, and all they that do not profess the Catholic Faith both in heart, word, and deed, that our Godfathers and Godmothers promised for us in Baptism. And all they that neglect to learn the Articles of our Faith and the Commandments of God. For we ought to learn the said Articles of our Faith and Ten Commandments before we receive the Blessed Sacrament of the Altar.

58. Who be they that break the First Commandment by doubting in Faith?

THEY that do not steadfastly believe, but doubt whether there be a Paradise, a Hell, and a Purgatory. Also they that do not steadfastly believe the Blessed Sacrament of the Altar and other Sacraments of the Catholic Church. For he that doubteth in Faith, mistrusteth the certainty of God's Word.

59. Who be they that break this Commandment by presumptuous searching of Faith?

THEY that presumptuously search the Articles of Faith; or doubting, dispute of Faith and Verity. And they that will believe

---

* Magical arts (see n. 63 below).

nothing concerning Faith but that which can be tried and shown by reason: for faith hath no merit where man's reason giveth experiment.[35] No man can try out his faith by reason.

60. Who breaketh the First Commandment by denying of Faith?

THEY that will not confess the Catholic Faith with their mouths, although they believe it in their hearts; for a Christian man ought to be of such constancy that he should rather suffer his life to be taken from him than his faith. And St. Paul saith: *we believe in heart to righteousness, and confess in mouth to salvation.*[36]

61. Who breaketh the First Commandment of God by tempting of God?

THEY that require miracles of God or of his Saints, and seek to be helped of God by miracle where they may be helped by other means. And they that for poverty, sickness, or adversity, do murmur and grudge that God will not grant them their desire, when peradventure they desire against their soul's health. For many times God doth not give us that which we desire, to the intent he may give us that which is better for us.

62. Who breaketh the First Commandment of God by unreverence of God?

THEY that do not give due reverence to God and his Saints, or to their Relics and Images. Secondly, they that unworthily receive the Blessed Sacrament of the Altar. Thirdly, they that unreverently behave themselves before the Blessed Sacrament. Fourthly, they that unreverently behave themselves in the Church, or other places dedicated to God's service; as they that will not pray with their mouths, kneel upon their knees, knock upon their breasts, hold up their hands and lift up their eyes when order requireth and necessity or reason dispenseth not.

63. Who breaketh the First Commandment by art Magik?

THEY that of purpose tell destinies by taking of lots or verses in the Scriptures, enchanters, witches, sorcerers, interpreters of dreams, and such like prohibited by the law of God; and all they that advisedly use their help to recover health, or to get a thing that is lost.

---

[35] Gregory the Great, *Homily 26 on the Gospels*
[36] Rom 10

64. How many ways is the First Commandment broken, concerning hope?

THREE manner of ways: By despair, by presumption of God's mercy, and presumption of our good works.

65. Who breaketh the First Commandment by despair?

FIRST, they that by temptation of the Devil, pusillanimity, or other infirmity destroy themselves upon mistrust of God's mercy.

Secondly, they that do think their sins so great, that God either cannot or will not forgive their sins. Thirdly, they that heap sin upon sin and will not go about to get remission of their sins. All such break this Commandment.

66. Who breaketh the First Commandment by presumption of God's mercy?

FIRST, they that continue in sin still, trusting to have mercy without Penance and everlasting life without good works; and will say God hath created them and redeemed them, and therefore he must needs save them. Secondly, they that trust only by Christ's Passion, or by only faith to be saved. Thirdly, they that continue in sin still, trusting in the hour of death to ask mercy and to have it—which is a presumption without all discretion. For when the heart is pinched with pangs of death, the body vexed with sickness, the mind tossed with the perplexity of hell-fire, and both body and soul environed and compassed about with horrible swarms of devils, then commonly grace and memory faileth to ask mercy. And then it fareth (as Scripture saith) *he that loveth danger, shall perish in it.*[37] For he that will not seek for mercy when he may, often lacketh it when he would have it. All such break the Commandment of God by presumption of God's mercy.

67. Who breaketh the First Commandment by presumption of good works?

ALL they that think their merits so great that they ought to have no adversity in this life, and that they shall possess heaven only by their merits. And they that think they can merit of themselves, without the continual grace of God. Such break the Commandment of God by presumption of good works.

---

[37] Sir 3

68. How many ways is the First Commandment broken, concerning Charity?

THREE manner of ways: by love of worldly things, by worldly fear, and by servile fear.

69. Who breaketh the First Commandment by love of worldly things?

FIRST of all they that love wife, child, master, friend, or themselves more than God. Secondly, they that for worldly gains, preferment, or carnal pleasure neglect their duty to God. Thirdly, they that be more careful for worldly things than for heavenly things, and would still remain in this world if they might. For the love of God and the world cannot dwell together in one heart. Nor can one heart serve God and Mammon. All such break the Commandment of God.

70. Who breaketh the First Commandment by worldly fear?

FIRST of all they that for fear of Princes, Lords, Magistrates or Masters, do not obey the Commandment of God. Secondly, they that fear more the displeasure of any man than of God. Thirdly, they that for fear to be talked of or scorned, withdraw themselves from Divine service or worshipping of God or of his Saints. Such break this Commandment of God.

71. Who breaketh the First Commandment by servile fear?

ALL they that keep the Commandments of God only for fear of punishment in hell-fire, and not for the love of God. All such break this Commandment of God.

72. How many causes be there that move us to love God above all things?

SEVEN especially:
1. God's chief goodness.
2. He loved us first.
3. He is our Father.
4. He hath redeemed us.
5. He provideth continually for us.
6. He is present unto us in the Blessed Sacrament.
7. He promiseth to us a reward that eye never saw, that ear never heard, that heart never thought.

Of the Second Commandment

73. What is the Second Commandment of God?
THOU shalt not take the Name of God in vain.

74. What meaneth this Commandment?
IT doth forbid and condemn the abusing and unreverent taking of the name of God and his Saints, or any creature; which is committed of perjurers and blasphemers.[38] No man may swear an oath without a great cause, and that must be before a Judge in verity, in justice, and judgment; that is, truly, uprightly, and advisedly. Otherwise all our talk ought to be "yea" and "nay."

75. How many ways is the name of God taken in vain?
FIVE manner of ways: By perjury, blasphemy, unlawful vows, breaking of lawful vows, and by unadvised taking of the name of God and his Saints.

76. How many ways is God offended by Perjury?
SEVEN manner of ways. First by falsity: in calling God or his Saints to witness, affirming with an oath that which is false, or that which we think to be false. Secondly by doubtfulness: affirming with an oath that which we be doubtful of, although it prove true afterward. Thirdly, if we promise with an oath to another that which we intend not to perform. Fourthly, if by craft or subtlety of words in an oath we go about to deceive the hearer's understanding. Fifthly, if we swear to do a naughty act or deed - which oath is not to be kept. Sixthly, if we swear to omit a good deed or work of Charity - which oath is not to be kept. Seventhly, if of purpose we compel any man to perjury.

77. How many ways is God offended by blasphemy?
SEVEN manner of ways. First, if we swear by false gods. Secondly, if we attribute unto God that which doth not agree to him; as to say God is not righteous or merciful. Thirdly, if we deny anything that agreeth to God; as to deny that God does take care of mortal things. Fourthly, if we attribute unto a creature that which only agreeth to God; as if we attribute to the Devil and fortune the power and dominion of all things. Fifthly, if we attribute members to God, as

---

[38] Sir 22; Mt 5

concerning his Divinity. Sixthly, if we curse God or his Saints, saying: God is not righteous if we may not have our own will. For as light is odious to sore eyes, and good meat unsavory to the sick, so God's mercy displeaseth evil and wicked people. Seventhly, if we do injury to God or to his Saints.

78. How many ways is God offended by unlawful vows?
FOUR manner of ways: First, if we make a vow to do an evil deed; as to kill a man or to maim him. Secondly, if we make a vow against a godly purpose; as not to enter into religion, or not to give alms. Thirdly, if we vow a lawful vow for an evil intent, that we may have our unlawful purpose - so as to make God the author of evil. Fourthly, if we make a vow that is foolish, indiscrete, or unreasonable. And if we do not perform our lawful vow in due time, we break God's Commandment. Yet some vows for a reasonable cause may be changed or dispensed with, by them that have authority to dispense.

Also, we may break the Second Commandment of God by unadvisedly taking of the name of God; as if without need or compulsion we swear in things that be certain, or if we swear of a perverse custom, or of purpose by God or his Saints in idle talk or anger. For he that is accustomed to swear cannot escape perjury.

Of the Third Commandment

79. What is the Third Commandment of God?
REMEMBER that thou sanctify and keep holy the Sabbath day.[39] In Moses' Law the people were commanded to sanctify and keep holy the Sabbath day, which day we call Saturday, or the seventh day. For after almighty God had created all kind of creatures in six days, the seventh day he rested or ceased to create any new creature. But in the law of grace we do not sanctify or keep holy the seventh day, called the Saturday: but we sanctify or keep holy the day following, called the Sunday or our Lord's Day; in the which day Christ our Lord arose from death, making mankind (that was created earthly) a heavenly creation, in the day of his resurrection.

This precept of sanctifying or keeping holy the Sunday, or our Lord's day, doth contain under it all feasts and holy days instituted and

---

[39] Ex 22

commanded by the Church. And we do sanctify the holy day, when we apply ourselves to the worshipping of God. Therefore upon Sundays and holy days we ought to search our conscience and purge it from sin: we should cry and call unto God for mercy and grace, thanking him for his manifold benefits bestowed upon us.[40] We ought to have in memory Christ's Passion, Paradise, Hell and Purgatory, so to abstain from sin and exercise ourselves in things that be godly for our soul's health; as in going to the Church, to pray devoutly, reverently to hear Mass, and other Divine service.

80. How many ways is the holy day broken?

FOUR manner of ways: By servile work, by omitting the worshipping of God, by unreverence of holy things, and by wanton or unlawful plays.

81. How is the holy day broken by servile work or labor?

IF upon Sundays or holy days we work, or cause other to work any servile labor that properly pertaineth to servants; as plowing, carting, digging, and such like, or do use handicrafts. However, for pity or necessity some things be permitted to be done upon holy days; as dressing of meat, preparing of a medicine, burying the dead, and such like. Also it is permitted upon holy days to exercise the liberal sciences; as to dispute or study, to sing or to play upon instruments. And if necessity do constrain to take a journey upon the holy day, it is permitted.

82. How is the holy day broken in omitting the worship of God?

IF every Sunday and holy day we be not present at Divine service, and if we do not hear wholly one Mass with a devout reverent mind; or if we do not say our Divine service that we be bound unto; if we be not confessed at Easter and receive the Sacrament. In omitting these and such like, we break the holy day.

83. How is the holy day broken by unreverence of holy things?

IF we hear Mass unreverently; as talking, walking, gazing, or occupying ourselves idly. And if we misuse the church or church yard, or pollute the same, or if we use anything forbidden by Christ or his Church, we break the holy day.

---

[40] Lev 23; Jer 17; Num 15

84. How is the holy day broken by plays, pastimes, or gaming?
IF we misspend the holy day in unthrifty games, as cards and dice for covetousness, or when we should be at Divine service; or if we use dancing for wantonness, or if we frequent taverns or bowling alleys, or if we use any dishonest place or company. By these ways and such like we break the holy day, and so offend God.

Of the Fourth Commandment

85. What is the Fourth Commandment of God?
HONOR thy Father and Mother, that thy days may be long upon earth.[41]

86. In what things doth the honor consist, that we must do to our Fathers and Mothers?
IN three things: In reverence, obedience, and succoring them.[42]

87. How must we reverence our Fathers and Mothers?
IN loving them, doing good to them, in praying for them, being afraid lest we should offend them in word or deed. In giving place to them, we must reverence them both in words and gesture.

88. How do we offend in not reverencing our parents?
FIRST, if we neglect our natural parents or kinsfolk being in poverty or misery; if we deride or scorn them, or stir them to anger; or if we desire their death for hatred towards them or for desire of inheritance, goods, or honor; and by such like, we break God's precept. Secondly, we break the Commandment of God if we do not reverence our Prelates, Bishops, ghostly Fathers, and other spiritual rulers and governors in Christ's Church that have cure and charge of souls.[43] For whosoever doth contemn, despise, or scorn either their carnal parents or spiritual fathers, be accursed of God; as Ham was for laughing at his father Noah.[44] Thirdly, we break this Commandment of God if we do not reverence our Godfathers and Godmothers, our superiors and elders both in age, gravity, wisdom, virtue and learning; or in office, authority and dignity.

---

[41] Ex 20
[42] Eph 6; Col 3
[43] Rom 13; Heb 13; 1 Pet 2
[44] Gen 9

89. In what things must we obey our parents?

IN all things appertaining to God or good manners, in things that be honest and lawful. We must obey them by the example of our Savior Christ, who was obedient to his parents. And as we be bound to obey our carnal parents, so we be bound to obey our Prelates, Bishops, and spiritual governors in Christ's Church; we are bound to obey their precepts, and firmly to keep their doctrine that they have taught us, for our soul's health.

We must diligently take heed that we be not carried away with any strange heretical doctrine, and that we entangle not ourselves in schism; steadfastly we must cleave and stick to the doctrine concerning Faith and Religion that hath been taught in Christ's Church by a succession of Pastors and Bishops coming lineally from the Apostles; whose doctrine is derived from the Apostles to this day, from one to another. Whosoever doth not obey these spiritual Fathers, doth greatly offend God.

90. In what things must we succor our parents?

IN comforting them, and ministering necessities to them. For if any be so unnatural that they will not comfort them when they be alive, and pray for them when they be dead, they break the Commandment of God. Also by this Commandment every man and woman is bound to pay truly their tithes to their Prelates, and all other debts and duties due unto others.

And as the children be bound to obey their parents, so fathers and mothers ought to give good example to their Children. But some parents seek so much to enrich their Children in worldly things, that they purchase everlasting damnation both to themselves and to their children. Such parents show themselves to care only for the body, and not for the soul. If they see their Children in poverty or misery, they lament; but to see their Children in sinful life they little pass thereof.[45]

Of the Fifth Commandment

91. What is the Fifth Commandment of God?

THOU shalt not kill. That is to be understood: Thou shalt not without just authority kill or hurt any man in body or in soul. And therefore both the Judge in the commonwealth doth lawfully put

---

[45] Eph 6

offenders to death or otherwise punish them bodily, and the Bishop doth lawfully excommunicate wicked or disobedient persons; for the preservation of peace and tranquility in the commonwealth, and in the Church.

92. How many ways do we break this Commandment?

TWELVE manner of ways: First, if we kill, hurt or maim willfully ourselves or any other; or if we command any man unjustly to be killed or hurt, or give counsel, aid, or help thereunto. Secondly, If women by medicine (as by herbs, drinks, or by any other means) kill their Children after their conception; or if any man kill the child in the mother's womb by strokes or by other means. Or if any man or woman procure barrenness to themselves or to any other. Thirdly, they break this Commandment that by witchcraft or by any such Devilish means be the cause of any man's death.

Fourthly, they that shorten their life by surfeiting with meats and drinks, or by riotous, wanton life. Fifthly, Princes and such as be in authority, if they make laws to put innocents or any man to death unjustly; as they that have made laws to put the holy Martyrs to death for confessing Christ and the Catholic Faith. Sixthly, They that of malice do wish hurt, death, or damnation to any man; or they that rejoice of any man's adversity or be sorry to hear of other men's felicity; or they that speak contumeliously of any man; or they that desire God to take vengeance upon any man or woman.

Seventhly, they that neglect to succor and help them that be in extreme necessity. Saint Ambrose doth say: "feed them that be like to die for hunger, for if thou do not feed, thou hast killed."[46] Eighthly, they that do imagine hurt or displeasure to any man; or make conspiracies or take counsel to imprison, vex, or trouble innocents or any man for a godly cause, as for the Catholic Faith or Religion. Ninthly, they that have offended any man and will not ask forgiveness; and they that will not forgive them which have offended, but will do evil for evil.

Tenthly, they that kill the souls of the people with heresy or wicked doctrine or counsel, whereby souls are brought to damnation; and they that corrupt youth with wicked doctrine, or by any means corrupt good manners. Eleventhly, they that show evil example in word or deed, and they that will not admonish their offending neighbor. Twelfthly, fathers, mothers, and schoolmasters, if they do

---

[46] Ambrose, as cited in Gratiam's *Decretum*, Can. 21, D. 86.

not correct offending children with the rod discretely; for he that spareth the rod, hateth the child (saith Solomon[47]); and they that will not correct offending children, kill their souls. By correcting children with the rod, fathers, mothers, and masters may deliver the children's souls from hell. Therefore it is better to be unborn than untaught. But in doing correction, anger must follow reason and be ruled by reason.

We must beware that we break not this Fifth Commandment of God in any of these twelve ways before said.

Of the Sixth Commandment

93. What is the Sixth Commandment of God?
THOU shalt not commit adultery.[48] Under this Commandment is forbidden all unlawful company in lechery: whether it be fornication between unmarried persons, deflowering of virgins, rape, incest between kinsfolk, sacrilege as pretended marriage of priests or between religious persons, or in sin against nature[*], which is most horrible in the sight of God.[49] Also they that be unlawfully married and inordinately give themselves to carnal lust - for the special cause of marriage ought to be for procreation of children.[50] And under this precept is also forbidden all consent in delectation and voluptuous pleasure of carnal concupiscence and lechery; as dishonest handling or touching themselves or others for lust or unlawful appetite, whereby nature is stirred or concupiscence kindled.

In like manner they sin that suffer others willingly and dishonestly to touch or handle them. Also by inordinate or lascivious kissing or clipping, by bawdy songs or dishonest talking, or by any dissolute behavior; as wanton and unchaste sight, dancing to the intent to procure wanton love, or to move any to filthy sin. Also they that be bawds, to bring any persons together to commit sin; or they that give counsel, aid, succor or help thereunto in word or in deed. Finally, if in our hearts we give a full and deliberate consent to filthy sin of the flesh which may come of unchaste sight or talking, or of filthy thoughts and imaginations; although we do not accomplish our filthy lust either in

---

[47] Prov 23
[48] Ex 20
[*] Following St. Paul (cf. Rom 1), classical theology refers to sodomy as the "sin against nature" or the "unnatural sin." See also paragraph n. 172 below.
[49] 1 Cor 6; Mt 5
[50] Eph 5; 1 Thess 4

deed or in words, yet we may offend deadly. By all these ways afore said we may break the Sixth Commandment of God, and so set ourselves in a damnable state.

94. What means must we use to avoid the filthy sin of the flesh?

FIRST we must consider that lechery corrupteth every age;[51] it confoundeth all the senses; it breaketh all order; it perverteth every degree; it assaulteth young and old, men and women, wise and simple, superiors and inferiors;[52] it weakeneth the body and killeth the soul; it loseth good fame and offendeth the neighbor; it loseth God and winneth the Devil; it dulleth the wit and maketh men beastly; of the temple and members of Christ[53] it maketh the temple and members of the Devil. Fornicators and unclean livers shall have no inheritance in the Kingdom of God,[54] but their portion and part shall be in the lake that burneth with fire and brimstone. Saint Jerome compareth lechery to hellfire, whose flame is pride, whose sparks are ungodly talk, whose smoke is infamy, whose end is poverty, misery and hellfire.[55]

Consider moreover, the more any man giveth himself to voluptuous carnal pleasure, willing to satisfy his filthy concupiscence, the more shall his desire increase and the less shall he be satisfied. It is but a moment that this filthy lust delighteth; but the painful torments due for the same be eternal in hellfire.

They that will avoid this filthy sin first must keep their hearts clean from idle, filthy thoughts by holy meditations on Christ and his Saints. Secondly, they must shut up their eyes from vain aspects and their ears from ungodly talk. Thirdly, they must shut up their mouths from all talk sounding to sin, and use devout prayer. Fourthly, they must chastise their bodies with abstinence and fasting, watching and exercising of some godly labor, and flee from idleness and evil company. So by the help of God's grace, this filthy, damnable sin may be avoided.

Of the Seventh Commandment

95. What is the Seventh Commandment of God?

---

[51] Innocentius
[52] Bernardus
[53] Eph 5
[54] Rev 21
[55] Hieronymus

03-13-2020		FDXSP01	
Qty.	Content ID	Description	Page Count
1	25609606	TRADIVOX	160

Printed, bound, and packed with care at Lulu.com

Have a question about your order? Reach our support team at www.lulu.com/support, or call us toll-free at 1-844-212-0689

Lulu Press, Inc.
627 Davis Drive
Suite 300
Morrisville, NC 27560

Shipment Summary

Received by:
Greg King
2424 Custis Road
Arlington, VA 22201   United States

THOU shalt commit no theft.[56] By this Commandment we are forbidden to take, keep, or occupy anything that is another man's against the right owner's will, by violence, fraud, or deceit.

96. How many ways do we break this precept?

SEVENTEEN ways:

First, by sacrilege, as robbing of Churches, taking anything away that is dedicated to God or to his Saints out of the Churches or hallowed place and putting it to profane use. Secondly by Simony, in buying or selling or making any simoniacal pact for spiritual gifts or ecclesiastical promotion; as patrons that nominate or give any ecclesiastical benefice or promotion for profit or gains[57] either to themselves, or to some friend of theirs. They also break this Commandment that obtain Holy Orders by giving of money or money's worth, and they that give money for any ecclesiastical promotion, or promise any part of their benefice or spiritual living to the intent to obtain any such spiritual living. Whosoever doth so give or receive any such spiritual living doth not only commit grievous sin, but ought to be deprived, and make restitution to the Church. Thirdly, by usury in lending money, to the intent to have the same sums of money again with gains either in money or money's worth.[58] All such usurers are bound to make restitution to the party. Yet he that is urged with great necessity and can help himself by no other means does not offend in borrowing money and promising gain.

Fourthly, by theft, spoiling, or robbing openly or secretly. Fifthly, by deceiving or defrauding, or by any means doing wrong to children during their nonage. Sixthly, by bargaining or buying anything of servants, or of any that have no authority to sell. Seventhly, they that will not pay their debts or wages that they owe to any man. Eighthly, they that use extortion, polling, or oppression of their subjects or tenants. Ninthly, scholars that receive money of their parties to buy necessities with, if they bestow it upon vanities instead. Tenthly, they that deceive any man in paying counterfeited money or gold for good and lawful, although they have received the same for good of others.

Eleventhly, they that hurt or destroy other men's goods, either openly or privily, and they that will not make a recompense for hurt done to their power. Twelfthly, they that are hired to work yet do not

---

[56] Ex 20
[57] Acts 8
[58] Psa 14

their work truly; and they are bound to make restitution of the damage and loss. Thirteenthly, they that retain or keep anything that they have found which another has lost by negligence against his will. For what thou hast found and not restored, thou hast stolen (if thou know the owner.)[59] And if by diligent search and inquisition thou canst not find the right owner, thou art bound to give unto the poor what thou hast found. Fourteenthly, they that use untrue weights or measures in buying or selling; or they that sell that for good which they know to be naught; or sell one thing for another, whereby the buyer is deceived; or in bargaining use crafty or subtle words.

Fifteenthly, they that use craft or deceit in gaining for covetousness - such are bound to make restitution. Sixteenthly, he that taketh an Action unjustly against any man for gains, or doth give counsel, aid, or consent; or they that praise any man in a naughty act, or they that hold their peace when they may prevent an evil deed, deceit, or unrighteousness to be done to any man. Seventeenthly, they that be in authority, if they do not make laws and provision to their power to repress all injuries, wrongs, and deceits before said; for in all these seventeen ways the Commandment of God is broken.

Of the Eighth Commandment

97. What is the Eighth Commandment of God?

THOU shalt bear no false witness against thy neighbor.[60]

First, by this Commandment is forbidden all hurtful lying, whether it be in judgment or in common and familiar talk, whereby hurt cometh to any man or woman. Secondly, it is forbidden to slander or to speak evil of any man, or to manifest the secret sin of any man. Thirdly, it is forbidden to dispraise or diminish the good deeds or acts of any man, to bring him out of favor or estimation. Fourthly, it is forbidden to use craft to hide the truth, being called in judgment to witness the truth.

Fifthly, it is forbidden to deride or scorn others with scornful words, or to object a crime to do displeasure to any man or woman. Sixthly, it is forbidden to detract or impair the good name or fame of any that is absent; whether they say true or false, they ought to restore their good name and fame. Seventhly, it is forbidden to take pleasure

---

[59] Augustine, Bk. 50 hom. Hom. 9 & de verbis Apost. serm. 19.
[60] Ex 20

to hear evil spoken of any man or woman, for every man ought to answer for his neighbor, to defend his good fame.[61] Eighthly, he doth offend God grievously, that doth defame or slander himself. Ninthly, they that curse themselves or others with evil words of mischief, or vengeance, or such like ungodly words; and also they that ask vengeance or mischief upon unreasonable creatures such as cattle, corn, ground, and such like, break God's precept.

Tenthly, it is forbidden to judge rashly, or to take or to interpret the words or deeds of any man in the worst part; for in things that be doubtful, we ought to judge the best. Eleventhly, it is forbidden to use whispering with contentious words to provoke any man to wrath, or to set dissension between party and party, or to cause dissension to continue. Twelfthly, it is forbidden to use flattery as to praise any man or woman of a deed that is deadly sin, or to praise any many or woman to the intent to hurt them in body or soul, or by flattering or praising to be the cause of deadly sin. Thirteenthly, it is forbidden to use dissimilation in words or deeds. Also, it is forbidden to break honest and lawful promises.

Fourteenthly, it is forbidden to hurt the souls of the people with heresy and false doctrine contrary to the Catholic Faith, whereby the people are deceived and brought into state of damnation.[62] Heretics bear false witness with the Devil against Christ and his dear spouse the Catholic Church.[63] They maintain falsity against the truth, and although they be punished or put to death by burning or otherwise, yet they receive no crown of martyrdom, but they receive punishment worthily for their infidelity and false witness against the truth. So heretics be children, martyrs, and witnesses for the Devil against Christ and his Church. Thus all manner of lies are to be detested and are forbidden by the Commandment of God.

Of the Ninth Commandment

98. What is the Ninth Commandment of God?
THOU shalt not covet or unlawfully desire thy neighbor's wife, maid, or daughter.[64] As in the Sixth Commandment, all carnal lust outwardly appertaining to the sin of the flesh is forbidden. So in this

---

[61] Eph 7
[62] 2 Pet 2
[63] Cyprianus
[64] Ex 20

precept is forbidden all inward concupiscence and unlawful carnal desire of thy neighbor's wife, daughter, or maid in heart and mind; for many are chaste in body that have committed adultery or lechery in will.[65] Christ saith in the Gospel: He that looketh upon a woman, coveting in his mind to commit carnal act with her, already in his heart he hath committed lechery with her. For although the thoughts be hidden from man and cannot be judged by man's law, yet all things that we imagine or think in our hearts are open and unhidden to the eyes of God. And the will and intent that is ready to commit sin is reputed before God as the fact and deed done, only being prevented against the will; for he that hath a full will to commit lechery if opportunity or time would serve, breaketh this Commandment.

Also they that be negligent to resist temptations or to repress and refrain the passions or concupiscence of the flesh, or suffer thoughts of carnality to continue with delectation in their minds; for everyone ought to defend their chastity as their lives. Finally, they that trim or deck themselves to allure and provoke others to their carnal love, or use flattery or dissimulation to provoke others to sin; all such break the Commandment of God.

Of the Tenth Commandment

99. What is the Tenth Commandment of God?

THOU shalt not covet thy neighbor's goods.[66] As in the Eighth Commandment the outward act of theft, damage, and hindrance is forbidden to be done to thy neighbor in his soul, body, or goods; so in this Tenth Commandment is forbidden the inward will and desire unjustly to have thy neighbor's goods. For they that refrain to take or keep their neighbor's goods only for fear of worldly punishment or shame, break this precept. And they that be ready in mind and will to put forth their money to usury, or to be in will to steal, to take any man's goods to keep them or hurt them, or to withhold anything that is found if opportunity of time would serve thereunto - all such break this Commandment. Also they that play at any game for the intent to get their neighbor's goods break this Commandment.

Also they that covet to have any ecclesiastical promotion, authority, and dignity by unlawful means, break this Commandment.

---

[65] Mt 5
[66] Ex 20, 1 Thess 4

No man may do evil to the intent that goodness may come thereof;[67] and much more grievously they offend God that desire goods, lands, dignities or promotion, to maintain their solace and worldly pleasure.

100. What is the sum of the Ten Commandments?

THE sum of the Ten Commandments doth consist in the love towards God and our neighbor.[68] In the First Table be three Commandments which take away and forbid sin and vice against the worshipping of God; they forbid idolatry, apostasy, heresy, superstition, perjury, blasphemy, and move us to the pure and true worshipping of God in heart, word, and deed. In the Second Table be seven Commandments, which command us to give reverence and honor to every man in his degree, to profit all and hurt none, to do unto others as we would be done to ourselves.

The Five Commandments of the Church

Ne dimittas legem matris.
Forsake not the law of thy mother.
(Prov 1)

101. How many Commandments be there of the Church that we be bound to keep?

THERE be five precepts especially Commanded by our mother the Catholic Church, Christ's dear Spouse, which we are bound to keep.[69] For if we should be disobedient children to our mother the Catholic Church and not obey her precepts, we cannot have God to be our loving Father.[70]

The first precept is that we celebrate and keep holy days commanded by the Catholic Church. As in the Old Testament the people were bound to celebrate diverse feasts beside the Sabbath day, so in the New Testament we are bound to celebrate diverse feasts besides the Sunday.[71]

The second precept is that every Sunday and holy day we reverently hear Mass.[72]

---

[67] Rom 3
[68] Eph 4; Mt 7
[69] Mar. I.
[70] Cyprian, *On the Unity of the Church*
[71] Concil. Lugd. Holy days.
[72] Mass. Concil. Agath.

The third precept is that we keep the fasting days commanded by the Church, and abstain from such meats as the Church doth prohibit and forbid.[73]

Fourthly, every man and woman once in the year is bound to be confessed of all their sins to their own Curate or to some discrete Priest that hath authority to absolve them of their sins.[74]

The fifth precept is that every man and woman having reason and discretion, once in the year at the least, receive the Blessed Sacrament of the Altar, and especially at Easter time.[75]

These and such like precepts of the Church we are bound to observe and keep. The observing of these precepts and such like is both profitable and necessary; First, for the exercise of our faith, humility, and Christian obedience. Secondly, because they nourish, keep and maintain godly worship, honest discipline, and public tranquility, and marvelously set forth all things in a decent order in Christ's Church. Thirdly, the charitable keeping of them bringeth everlasting life; but the contemning of these precepts and such like of Holy Church bringeth everlasting damnation.

The Five Senses

Exhibete membra vestra servire iustitiae, in sanctificationem.
Bestow your members to serve justice for sanctification.
(Rom 6)

102. How many outward senses hath God given to us?

FIVE: Sight, Hearing, Smelling, Tasting, and Touching; the which Senses we ought to use to the honor of God, to the health of our souls, and the necessary use of our bodies. And except with great diligence we keep and refrain the said outward Senses, they be as open windows for sin and death to enter in at, to our souls.

God hath given to us our eyes that we may **see** to flee from such things as be hurtful either to our bodies or to our souls, and keep such things as be good and necessary. And as this sense of sight is more excellent than other senses, so is it more perilous: for except our sight be restrained and ruled by reason, it doth allure and entice us to

---

[73] Can. Apost. 68.
[74] Concil. Later. Confession.
[75] Concil. Later.

many sins. First, they offend God by sight that take pleasure to look upon their own comeliness of body or clothing and such like. And they that with proud looks turn their eyes from place to place. They also, that give their eyes unchastely to look upon any - for a wanton and unchaste eye is a sign of an unchaste heart and mind. And they that idly behold the gesture or gait of any. And they that seeing another man's felicity, be sorry; or seeing another man's calamity, rejoice. And they that for hatred, disdain to look upon any man. And they that seeing another man's goods, desire the same. And they that take pleasure to look upon filthiness or any ungodliness. All such as are before spoken of, misspend their sense of sight and commit sin.

God hath given to us our ears, to **hear** such things as be good and honest. God being a marvelous craftsman, would that man should have two ears and but one tongue; to the intent he should hear more than he should speak. Our ears are given to us to perceive the doctrine of God, for our soul's health. All these ways following, we do misspend our sense of hearing, and so offend God: If we be angry (more than reason doth permit) when we hear anything that does not please us. If we take pride to hear our own praise. If we take pleasure to hear lascivious or wanton talk, scoffing, flattering, or slanderous words. If we take pleasure to hear heresy or Devilish doctrine.

God hath given to us the sense of **smelling**, whereof the nose is an instrument to draw sweet smells to the brain that be profitable to the body and not hurtful to the soul. These ways following, we may misspend the sense of smelling: If inordinately we be delighted with the pleasant smell of delicious meats, desiring the same. If for lasciviousness or voluptuousness, we be delighted with sweet odors, ointments, powders or perfumes. If we abhor the poor or sick and be over careful, least we should feel the odor or smell of them.

God hath given to us the sense of **tasting**, whereof the tongue is an instrument to taste or discern savor or taste in such things as be for the nourishment of the body, and not hurtful to the soul. This sense of tasting, except it be ruled by reason, brings many infirmities to the body and is cause of sin. We do misspend this sense of tasting by surfeits of meats or drunkenness, or being overmuch delighted in delicious meats and drinks. And in breaking fasting days, or in eating flesh or other meats for deliciousness, at such times as the Church doth prohibit and forbid the same.

God hath given to us the sense of **touching**, which consisteth in all parts of the body but especially in the hands; for there is a multitude of veins and sinews come together. This sense is given to us that we should use it to the profit of our bodies and souls. We do misspend this sense of touching if in malice we kill, wound, or strike any man; if we steal, rob, or take anything unjustly; if we unchastely touch ourselves or any other.

And as we do misspend these five sense, so we do misuse other parts of our bodies, and let sin enter into our souls.

Chapter 4

Sapientia cedisicauit sibi domum, and excidit septem columnas.
Wisdom hath built her an house, and hath cut out seven pillars.
(Prov 5)

103. What is a Sacrament?

A SACRAMENT is a visible form of an invisible grace, which is instituted of God for our sanctification.[76] In every Sacrament is an outward form or manner that we may see with our corporal eyes, under the which lieth hidden an invisible grace that we cannot see with our corporal eyes, which we must firmly believe.[77] As in Baptism we see the Child washed in water, and we hear the words of Baptism spoken, but invisibly the grace of the Holy Ghost doth purge the Child from sin; so the flesh is washed, that the soul may be purged.

104. How many Sacraments did Christ institute?

SEVEN, which be expressed in the Scripture; and they have continually been kept in the Catholic Church and used by tradition from the Apostles, from man to man, until these our days.[78] The sacraments be these: Baptism, Confirmation, Penance, the Sacrament of the Altar, Extreme Unction, Order, and Marriage - the which concerning the invisible grace that they give to the worthy receivers of them, take their efficacy and strength of the merits of Christ's Passion.

105. Why did Christ institute these seven Sacraments?

CHRIST did institute the Sacraments for four causes: First, to be medicines and preservatives against sin. Secondly, to be means and helps to the keeping of the Commandments of God. Thirdly, to induce us to humility and obedience, to bring us to knowledge and exercise of virtue in the fear of God. Fourthly, to be instruments or vessels whereby God doth pour abundantly his mercy and grace into our souls, and maketh us apt to receive the fruit and benefits of his Passion.

---

[76] Augustine, *On Christian Doctrine*, Bk. 3
[77] Ambrose, *On the Mysteries*, Ch. 3
[78] Council of Florence, Council of Trent

Of the Sacrament of Baptism

106. What is Baptism?

BAPTISM is the most necessary Sacrament of the New Testament, instituted of Christ specially to wash away original sin and all other sin done before Baptism.[79] By baptism we be regenerated and born again of water and the Holy Ghost, and made Children of God by adoption and heirs of the Kingdom of heaven. Without Baptism, either in act or in will, none can be saved.

107. What is the effect of Baptism?

THE effect of this Sacrament is to wash away all manner of sin so clean, that no satisfaction is to be enjoined. For if any die after Baptism, before they commit sin, their souls go straight to heaven.[80]

108. In what things doth Baptism consist?

IN two things especially: the matter and form. The matter is water, a simple element.[81] No Baptism can be in wine, rosewater, or any confect liquour. The form is the words of Baptism, which are: *Ego te baptiso in nomine Patris, et Filii, et Spiritus Sancti*: or "I Christen thee, in the name of the Father, and the Son, and the Holy Ghost. Amen."

109. Who is the minister of this Sacrament?

ORDINARILY the priest is the minister of the Sacrament of Baptism; but in time of necessity, a deacon or a layman; and in the absence of a man, a woman may baptize; or for lack of other an heretic or pagan may Christen - so long as they keep the form and have the matter, having an intent to do that which the Catholic Church doth. But it is to be noted that the minister, when he dippeth the Child in the water, or putteth water upon the head, which is the principal part of the Child, at the same instant time must speak the words of Baptism. If any layman or woman take upon them to Christen a Child, except it be in peril of death (when a Priest cannot be had), they offend God grievously in the sin of presumption.

110. Whether may one be Christened twice?

ONE Person can be Christened but once. Baptism cannot be iterated in any one Person, for Baptism doth impress and give a

---

[79] Jn 3; Rom 6; Gal 3
[80] Council of Florence
[81] Council of Florence

Character or a distinct spiritual sign that cannot be done away.

111. What do Godfathers and Godmothers for Children in Baptism?

GODFATHERS and Godmothers become sureties for children, and doth promise in the Children's name that they shall forsake the Devil, and all his works and pomps. Godfathers and Godmothers also become sureties for Children, and promise that they shall believe all the Articles of the Creed. Therefore Godfathers and Godmothers ought diligently to look to their charge when Children come to years of discretion, to bring them up spiritually, to teach them, or cause them to be taught the Catholic Faith and *Pater Noster*.

112. Why be ceremonies used in Baptism?

CEREMONIES be used in baptism partly against the power of the Devil, partly for instruction both of us and of them that be baptized.

113. Why be Exorcisms done over the child outside the Church?

FOR because before the child be Christened, he is no part of Christ's Catholic Church.

114. What profit hath the child by the Exorcisms?

BY the exorcisms the Devil is driven away, which goeth about to prevent the child from Baptism.

115. Why is the sign of the Cross made upon the child?

THE flesh is signed and crossed, that the soul may be armed and defended.[82] The sign of the cross is made in the child's forehead, which is a place of shamefacedness, that the child should never be ashamed to confess the Faith of Christ. The sign of the cross is made upon the child's breast, steadfastly to believe the Faith of Christ. The sign of the cross is made in the child's hand, to bless itself and defend itself from the Devil and all adversities, and to abide in the Catholic Faith.

116. Why is Salt put into the child's mouth?

THE Salt doth signify heavenly wisdom given to the Child by the Holy Ghost, to be used with discretion.

---

[82] Tertullian

117. Why doth the priest put spittle into the Child's ears and nose?

THE Priest doth put spittle into the child's ears and nose after the example of Christ healing a deaf man by putting his fingers in his ears, by spitting and touching his tongue;[83] that the child's ears may be open to hear wholesome doctrine, and to savor and taste that which is godly.

118. Why doth the Priest anoint the child with holy Oil upon the breast and back?

THE child is anointed upon the breast with holy Oil to signify that the Holy Ghost should always dwell in that heart and breast by faith and charity. The child is anointed upon the back with holy Oil to signify the yoke of our Lord, which is sweet and light.

119. Why is the child anointed with holy Chrism?

THE anointing of the child with holy Chrism on the head doth signify that thereby the child is incorporated into Christ, the Head of the mystical body of the Church; and of holy Chrism and Christ we take the name of Christians. So the flesh is anointed, that the soul may be consecrated and hallowed to everlasting life.

120. What doth the Chrism signify?

THE chaste garment of innocence and cleanness of a new life.

121. What doth the candle signify?

THE light of our good works that we must keep diligently, to enter in with the five wise virgins when Christ shall come to the marriage.[84]

Of the Sacrament of Confirmation

122. What is Confirmation?

CONFIRMATION is a Sacrament whereby the grace that was given in Baptism is confirmed and made more strong by the seven

---

[83] Mt 7
[84] Mt 25

gifts of the Holy Ghost.[85] For although the visible sign of the Holy Ghost that was manifestly seen in the Apostles' time doth now cease, yet the same grace invisible is given in Confirmation.[86]

123. In what things doth the substance of this Sacrament consist?
THE substance of this Sacrament consisteth in the matter and the form. The matter is holy Chrism[87], confect and made of oil olive and balm, consecrated of a Bishop; and every year it is renewed and the old Chrism burned. The oil doth signify the cleanness of conscience by the infusion of grace, and the fervent zeal of charity toward the maintenance of Christ's Faith, wherewith he is endued that is Confirmed. The balm doth signify the odor of good fame and also the sweetness of God's Holy Spirit, wherewith Christ doth allure and draw us to his service. The form is the words of Confirmation that the Bishop doth speak, when he maketh the sign of the Cross upon the forehead with holy Chrism.

124. Who is the minister of this Sacrament of Confirmation?
THE Bishop is the minister, and no inferior; and this Sacrament may not be iterated.

125. What is the effect of this Sacrament?
IN this Sacrament the Holy Ghost is given to make them that be confirmed more strong in grace. As the Holy Ghost was given to the Apostles in the day of Pentecost, so in Confirmation grace is given, boldly to confess the name of Christ and all things belonging to a Christian man. Therefore whosoever is confirmed hath a Cross made in his forehead with holy Chrism, where is the seat of shamefacedness - lest he should be ashamed to confess Christ and that he is a Christian.

126. What Ceremonies be used in Confirmation?
FIRST, he or she that cometh to be Confirmed must have one godfather or one godmother (that is already confirmed) to hold them up to the Bishop. Secondly, they that receive Confirmation have a blow on the cheek given to them of the bishop, in remembrance that they must suffer patiently and gladly rebukes and tribulation for the name of Christ and righteousness' sake. Thirdly, they that receive

---

[85] Acts 8; Council of Florence
[86] Acts 19
[87] Council of Florence

Confirmation, for the space of three days ought to have and bear about with them a band, in signification that Christ lay three days in his sepulcher; and upon the third day they that be confirmed must be brought to the Priest, and then in the holy place the Priest washeth off that chrism with salt and water, and burneth the band, casting the ashes in the churchyard. In some countries they use to tie the band upon the forehead of them that be Confirmed, where the bishop made the sign of the Cross with holy Chrism. In England they use to tie the band about the child's neck, and upon the third day the Priest looseth the band, and therewith washeth off the holy Chrism with holy water.

Of the Sacrament of Penance

127. What is Penance?

PENANCE is a Sacrament whereby a penitent sinner is purged, absolved, and made clean from sin.[88] For if any commit deadly sin after Baptism, the only refuge is to the Sacrament of Penance; without which Sacrament in act or in will, they that have committed mortal sin cannot be saved.[89]

128. What is the matter of this Sacrament?

THE matter of the Sacrament of Penance is the humble and true confession of a penitent sinner that is contrite in heart for the sin committed, plainly confessing before the Priest (sitting in God's stead) the sin done, being in will and mind not to commit sin again, and being content to do satisfaction by the appointment of his ghostly Father.

129. What is the form of this Sacrament?

THE form of the Sacrament of Penance is the words of absolution that the Priest speaketh over the sinner, by virtue of the which the Holy Ghost worketh remission and forgiveness of sin so that the sinner (being penitent) is purged and made clean from sin as he was in Baptism; saving that the penitent sinner after confession must do penance, or suffer pains for his sin either in this life or in Purgatory.

130. How many parts of Penance be there?

THREE: Contrition in heart, Confession with mouth to a ghostly Father, and Satisfaction in works; so that whosoever will be

---

[88] Jn 20
[89] Council of Florence

purged and made clean from sin must be sorry in heart for the sin done, willing to offend no more, and then plainly confess the sin with the circumstances thereof: as how often, the place, the time, age and degree of persons, naming none by name. These circumstances may alter and change the kind and nature of the sin; they may aggravate or diminish the sin. Thirdly, the sinner must bring forth fruit of penance by the appointment of his ghostly Father.

131. Who is the minister of this Sacrament?
THE priest is the minister, whose office is to hear the Confession and then to discern between sin and sin; to give counsel how to avoid the occasion of sin; and thereupon to enjoin penance and to pronounce the words of absolution over the penitent's sins.

132. How many manner of sins may be forgiven by this Sacrament?
TWO manner of sins: deadly sin, and venial. But deadly sin cannot be forgiven without this Sacrament, in deed or in will. Venial sin may be purged by prayer, almsdeeds, by the worthy receiving of the Blessed Sacrament of the Altar, by taking of holy water, knocking upon the breast, with holy meditation, the Bishop's blessing, and such like.

133. How shall we discern deadly sin from venial sin?
DEADLY sin so much displeaseth God, that thereby we be separated from God and charity,[90] in such sort that dying therein without this Sacrament of penance in act or in will, it bringeth everlasting damnation.[91] The Scripture noteth that all fornicators, adulterers, unclean livers, thieves, robbers, extortioners, oppressors, unlawful covetous persons, common drunkards, slanderers, wicked speakers, idolaters, unbelievers, witches, sorcerers, they that be malicious enemies, contentious persons, brawlers and chiders, dissentious persons, they that make sects or divisions, manslayers, and they that deny God for fear of man: these and such like commit deadly sin. And dying therein without Penance, they shall have no inheritance in the kingdom of heaven, but their portion and part shall be in the lake that burneth with fire and brimstone.[92]

In the foresaid sins we may offend deadly in three ways. In deeds or acts, as in satisfying our malice, contempt, or inordinate

---

[90] Eph 5
[91] Phil 3; Col 3
[92] Rev 21

concupiscence in the sins before said. In words, by advisedly expressing our malice or concupiscence in the sins before said. In our thoughts, by imagining with consent, by deliberation and delectation, any evil or displeasure to any man or giving full consent with deliberation to the suggestion of the Devil and carnal concupiscence, where the will and intent is counted for the deed of deadly sin before God.[93]

Venial sin is committed by acts and deeds, wherein is neither malice nor contempt, but curiosity or vanity; as idle words and thoughts without consent of evil. By venial sin we be not destitute of grace, nor separated from subjection to God, nor do we lose our Charity; but yet thereby our souls be darkened and we are made less apt to any good work, and a temporal pain is due for venial sin - either in this life, or in Purgatory if we be not purged by such means as God and holy Church hath ordained for the same. But exactly to determine and judge of venial sin appertaineth to God, and not to man.

134. What is the effect of the Sacrament of Penance?

THE effect of the Sacrament of Penance is to purge a sinner and absolve him from all sin, to restore him to the Church, to reconcile him to God; to enrich him with spiritual gifts, and of the child of the Devil to make him the child of God.

135. How must they behave themselves that would be confessed?

THEY must humbly kneel down at the Priest's feet and make the sign of the Cross upon their breast, and bless themselves in the Name of the Father, and the Son, and the Holy Ghost, and then say, *Benedicite*. And when the priest hath given them a benediction, they must begin to acknowledge themselves sinners to God, our Lady Blessed Mary, with all the holy company of heaven, before their ghostly father sitting in God's stead. Then they must plainly express and declare their sins committed in thought, word, and deed, in breaking the Commandments of God; and how they have offended in the seven deadly sins and branches of the same, in misspending the five outward senses, in not fulfilling the seven works of mercy bodily and ghostly. These things with the circumstances declared, the Priest will give the penitent sinner counsel how to avoid sin, and upon Penance enjoined, give him absolution.

---

[93] Mt 21; Mt 16

136. Whether may every Priest hear confessions and give absolution?

ALTHOUGH every Priest in extreme necessity may hear confessions and give absolution, yet such priests as be heretics or excommunicated, suspended or condemned ordinarily, may not loose, nor bind. Every man and woman is bound to be confessed of their own proper curate, except either by license of their own curate or otherwise they have license from the Bishop or superior authority to choose them a discrete Priest to be their ghostly Father.[94]

137. Whether may every Curate of his ordinary authority absolve from every sin?

NO. For there be some sins so grievous that none may absolve but the Pope or his Legate: as burning of Churches, violent striking a Priest, and counterfeiting of the Pope's Letters or Bulls. Some sins appertain to the Bishop or his Penitentiary to absolve: as incest between kinsfolk, deflowering of virgins, manslaughter, breakers of vows, perjurers, witches, sorcerers, robbers of Churches, they that strike their Fathers or Mothers, Sodomites, burners of houses, they that overly their Children, blasphemers, heretics, adulterers, and such like. Whosoever hath committed any of these ought to go to the Bishop or to his Penitentiary for absolution.

138. How often in the year is every man and woman bound to go to Confession?

EVERY man and woman is bound (at the least) once in the year (at Lent) to go to Confession; and as often as they receive the Blessed Sacrament of the Altar, if they know or suspect themselves to be in deadly sin.[95]

139. Whether is any man or woman bound to iterate and confess again any sins that they have once confessed to a Priest?

IN three cases we are bound to iterate and confess again our sins. First, if the Priest that we were confessed of lacked authority to absolve such sins as we had done. Secondly, if the Priest that we were confessed of lacked discretion and knowledge to discern and judge our sins. Thirdly, if we have divided our Confession, showing part to one

---

[94] Lateran Council
[95] Council of Florence

Priest and part to another, by means whereof our ghostly father could not plainly understand our sins with the circumstances.

Of the Sacrament of the Altar

140. What is the Sacrament of the Altar?

IT is a Sacrament wherein is contained the Body and Blood of our Savior Christ, which is consecrated upon an Altar by a lawful Priest at Mass.[96]

141. What is the matter of this Sacrament?

THE matter of this Sacrament is bread of wheat and wine of the vine mixed with water; which doth signify the joining of the people to Christ, and also it doth signify the blood and water that did flow out of Christ's side when he was pierced to the heart with a spear.

142. What is the form of this Sacrament?

THE form of this Sacrament is the words of Christ wherewith this Sacrament is made, for the Priest speaketh in person of Christ. By virtue of the words of Consecration the substance of bread is turned and changed into the very Body of Christ, and the substance of wine is turned into the Blood of Christ, the Holy Ghost working by a divine power; so that Christ is wholly under the form of bread, and in every part of the Host being broken, Christ is wholly. Also under the form of wine, and every part thereof being separated, Christ is wholly.[97]

143. What is the effect of this Sacrament?

THE effect of this Sacrament is to knit, join, and incorporate the worthy receivers thereof unto Christ.[98] By the worthy receiving of this Blessed Sacrament grace is increased, virtue is nourished, steadfastness is given against frailty, strength against temptation, the merits of Christ's Passion are revived in us. Our bodies and souls are spiritually nourished with this Blessed Sacrament (being the blessed fruit of holy Mary) to be a medicine, to expel the poison that came to all mankind by the fruit that our first parent tasted of in Paradise. As that fruit brought everlasting death and damnation, so this Blessed

---

[96] Mt 16; 1 Cor 11; Lateran Council
[97] Lateran Council
[98] Council of Florence

Sacrament is a pledge to bring us to everlasting life, and to restore us to the joy that was lost by our first parents.

144. Who is the minister of this Sacrament?

THE Minister is a priest lawfully ordained and consecrated by a Bishop. It is required that the Priest do consecrate at Mass, having an intent to consecrate the Body and Blood of Christ.

145. Who is bound to receive this Sacrament?

EVERY Christian man and woman having discretion that is twelve years of age and elder is bound at every Easter time to receive, and at other times as their devotion will serve them.[99] In the primitive Church the people used often to receive, as every Sunday. Afterward devotion began something to decay, that customarily the people received three times in the year, as at Christmas, Easter, and Pentecost. Then afterward devotion waxed so very cold, that it was thought good to the Church to make a law that every man and woman upon pain of deadly sin should receive the Blessed Sacrament at Easter time at the least. And it is convenient that every Christian man and woman against death receive this Sacrament, to be their voyage provision.

146. How ought every man and woman to prepare themselves to receive the Blessed Sacrament?

FIRST, they ought diligently to examine their own conscience,[100] and if they perceive any deadly sin in them, with a penitent heart they ought to confess their sin to a discrete ghostly Father that hath authority to absolve them from their sins. So having their conscience purged from sin and with a fervent and reverent devotion, worshipping Christ in the Blessed Sacrament, they may safely receive. For as the benefit is great in the worthy receivers, so the unworthy receivers receive their own damnation.

Of the Sacrament of Extreme Unction

147. What is the Sacrament of Extreme Unction?

EXTREME Unction or Anointing is a Sacrament wherein the sick persons (by Holy Oil and the words of Christ) are relieved, that

---

[99] Lateran Council
[100] 1 Cor 11

more happily they may depart out of this world and also that their bodies may be restored to health, if it be expedient.[101] This Sacrament is to be ministered to men and women lying in extreme sickness in peril of death by God's visitation, and not by violence of war or execution. And this Sacrament is not to be ministered unto infants and such as lack reason; for none ought to receive this Sacrament but such as have reason and humbly desire it for God's sake.

148. What is the matter of this Sacrament?

THE matter is olive oil hallowed by a Bishop, wherewith the sick is anointed upon the eyes, ears, mouth, nose, hands, and feet. A man is anointed upon the reins of the back, and a woman upon the belly, because concupiscence reigneth most in those parts.

149. What is the form of this Sacrament?

THE form is the words that the Priest speaketh, when he doth anoint the sick in the foresaid parts or places.

150. What is the effect of this Sacrament?

THE effect of this Sacrament of Anointing is to put away and purge venial sin committed by misspending of our senses, and to purge and put away sins forgotten.[102] This Sacrament is comfortable to the soul, and healthful to the body as much as is expedient. And in this Sacrament the Holy Ghost doth strengthen the sick with grace against the violent assaults of the Devil and the terror of death.

151. Who is the Minister of this Sacrament of Extreme Unction or Anointing?

THE Priest is the Minister of this Sacrament, whom the sick ought to send for; and before he receives this Sacrament, he ought to be confessed of his mortal sins and receive absolution of the Priest, and also the Sacrament of the Altar, and humbly desire the Priest for God's sake to be anointed.

152. How should the Priest anoint them that lack eyes, hands, or any such parts as should be anointed?

THE Priest must anoint the parts that be there next adjoining unto these parts that should be anointed; for although any lack such parts wherewith they may offend outwardly, notwithstanding they have

---

[101] Jas 5; Council of Florence
[102] Council of Florence

those members grounded in the soul and all things due thereunto them; whereby they may offend inwardly about those things that appertain to those members, although outwardly they cannot be expressed.

Of the Sacrament of Order

153. What is the Sacrament of Order?

ORDER is a Sacrament, wherein grace or a spiritual power is given to Priests and to other ministers in their Consecration by the outward sign of imposition of the Bishop's hands, to exercise effectually the ministration of the Church; as in ministering of Sacraments, preaching, and exercising of discipline.[103] And whatsoever they do in the Church, according to the institution of Christ and his Church, almighty God doth ratify, accept, and allow. Therefore all people of whatsoever degree, estate, or authority they be, ought to obey the Bishops and Priests in causes Ecclesiastical. This is a power of the Church, given to them that be lawfully ordained and consecrated, which power is not by laws of men or of nature, but only of Christ above nature.

154. What is the matter of this Sacrament?

THE matter is that thing by delivering of which Order is given[*] - as Priesthood is given or delivered by giving of the chalice and paten with bread and wine. Deaconship is given by delivering of a book of the Gospels. Subdeaconship is given by the empty chalice and paten. And in like manner the inferior Orders have some special matter appertaining to their Order; as the giving of the keys to the Ostiary or Porter, the book to the Exorcist, the book of Psalms and Prophets to the Reader called Lector, the candle and cruet to the Acolyte.

---

[103] Council of Florence; Mt 10; 1 Tim 3; Tit 3; Acts 1

[*] The essential matter required for valid sacramental ordination was given further precision under Pope Pius XII (cf. *Sacramentum Ordinis*, 1947) as being specifically the *impositio manus* (laying on of hands), long occurring in the Roman Rite amid the conferral of liturgical instruments (*traditio instrumentorum*) as described here.

155. What is the form of this Sacrament?

THE form is the words of Order which the Bishop speaketh, whereby an authority is given to exercise some office in the Church; as in Priesthood the formal words be: *Accipe potestatem offerendi Sacrificium, Missasque celebrandi, tam pro viuis, quam pro defunctis, in nomine Domini.* By these words, the Bishop giveth authority and power to him that receiveth Priesthood to offer Sacrifice, and to celebrate Mass both for them that be alive and for them that be dead, in the Name of our Lord.

Whosoever shall receive the Order of Priesthood must by degrees receive six orders before of the Bishop; of the which Orders four be called Inferior Orders: Exorcists, which have authority given to them to expel devils from them that be possessed. Ostiaries (or Porters) have authority to keep the Church door, to expel the unworthy, and to let into the Church the faithful and worthy. Readers (called Lectors) have authority to read lessons and scriptures in the Church; whereby the understanding of the faithful people is lightened. Acolytes have authority to bear cruets to the Altar with wine and water, and to bear candles and tapers; wherewith the mind of the people may be kindled and stirred to devotion.

These four Orders have not continence so annexed unto them but that they may marry. Subdeacon, Deacon, and Priest have continence so annexed to their Orders that they may not marry.

Subdeacon hath authority to read the Epistle, to prepare necessities for ministration, and to assist the Priest in ministration. Deacon hath authority given to him from God by the Bishop to read the Gospel, and to assist the Priest in ministration of the Sacraments and other offices in the Church. The Priest hath his hands sanctified and hallowed by the bishop to sanctify and bless. And authority is given from God by the Bishop to the Priest to minister Sacraments, that is:

Baptism, whereby people first enter into the Church of God.

Secondly, if after Baptism any man fall into deadly sin, the Priest hath authority to absolve them, if with a contrite heart they confess their sin before him.

Thirdly, the Priest hath authority to consecrate and minister the Sacrament of the Altar.

Fourthly, the Priest hath authority to pray over the sick persons and to anoint them with Holy Oil in the Name of God, to the remission of their sins and to the salvation of the sick, according to God's pleasure.

Fifthly, the Priest hath authority to join those two persons together in Matrimony that marry in Christ.

156. What doth the Crown signify?

IT doth signify that they should be as kings, to rule and govern spiritually both themselves and others. The shaving of the hairs upon the crown of the head doth signify the renouncing and putting away of earthly affections and the lifting up of their minds toward heaven, making themselves heirs of God, that they may have their portion and part with God. The round circle of the crown doth signify perfection of life.

157. How many things do prevent the reception of Orders?

FIRST, a woman may not take Orders, nor a child, nor any that lacketh discretion; but he must be a man of full age, that shall take Holy Orders. Secondly, a servant that is in bondage to his Master may not take Holy Orders without his Master's consent - for if he do, his Master may compel him to do his service. Thirdly, a manslayer in deed or consent may not take Holy Orders. Fourthly, he that is not legitimate may not take Holy Orders without a dispensation. Fifthly, he that is married may not take Holy Orders (for continence is annexed to Holy Order) except by consent of his wife, who must vow chastity. Sixthly, he that is *Bigamus*, which hath married two wives and known them both carnally; or he that hath married a widow or a woman that is corrupt of another, if after carnally he know her; or if he carnally company with his own wife after that she hath committed adultery with another man; such a man may not take Holy Orders. Seventhly, he that lacketh any member or hath defect or deformity may not take Holy Orders. Eighthly, he that is infamed; or a slanderous person having any notorious crime, may not take Holy Orders.

158. Who is bound to say Canonical hours daily?

HE that is within Holy Orders is bound to say Canonical hours. For canonical hours - as Matins, Prime, and Hours, Evensong, and Compline, with other divine service - be annexed to Holy Orders to give God thanks. Also they that be beneficed be likewise bound. If for negligence or sloth any do omit their divine Service, they offend God.[104]

159. Who is the minister of this Sacrament of Order?

THE Bishop ordinary is the Minister.

160. What is the effect of Order?

THE effect of the Sacrament of Order is to give increase of grace by the imposition of the Bishop's hands, whereby one may be a meet minister in the Church of God.[105]

Of the Sacrament of Matrimony

161. What is Matrimony?

MATRIMONY, which is a sign of the conjoining of Christ and the Church his Spouse, is a Sacrament whereby man and woman lawfully joined together in marriage do enter into an undivided society of fellowship of life; and grace is given therein, both honestly and Christianly to procreate children and to bring them up godly, and also to avoid filthy lust and incontinency.[106]

162. What is the efficient cause of Matrimony?

THE efficient cause is a mutual consent of the man and woman expressed by words of matrimony at the time present, when the man saith: I take thee to my wife, and the woman saith: I take thee to my husband. And therein ought of necessity to be the presence of witnesses, and of congruity, the consent of friends.

163. Whether may a man put away his wife for any cause?

A MAN may put away his wife for no cause, except for fornication only;[107] and if for that cause any be separated at bed, neither of them may marry any other as long as both they live. For Matrimony is a perpetual bond of a lawful Contract or Marriage.

164. At what age may marriage be made?

---

[104] Lateran Council
[105] Council of Florence
[106] Gen 10; Mt 19; 1 Cor 7; Eph 5
[107] Mt 19

SPOUSAGE may be at seven years of age, but full consent in Marriage must not be before the woman be twelve years of age, and the man fourteen years of age.

165. Whether doth carnal copulation after Spousage or truthplight, make Matrimony?

IF carnal copulation follow the spousage or truthplight, with this mind to be one to the other as man and wife, it maketh Matrimony: but if it be for the intent of fornication, it is no Matrimony.

If man and woman bind themselves by faith and troth, or by book oath, with mutual consent to marry either other in time to come; although thereby they be bound to marry, upon pain of setting themselves in a damnable state yet lacking the formal word of Matrimony, it is no Marriage.

If either of them marry any other after the former promise, they must so continue and not be separated. For although they spake words of promising marriage in time to come, the words of the time present must take place.

If man and woman with a mutual consent in heart shall speak some words of the time to come, thinking thereby that they be made man and wife before God, it standeth for Marriage; but not before man and the Church's judgment, which must judge upon the words, and not upon the mind and intents. And if either of them marry any other, they live in adultery.

Whereas holy Church hath ever detested and forbidden privy contracts, yet when any such have been done with consent and formal words, it hath been marriage before God; whether they have had witness or not. Albeit this matter of privy Contracts, being thoroughly examined at the last general council held at Trent, the inconvenience that did arise thereof diligently weighed and considered; for the better safeguard of the peoples' consciences and avoiding contention, it was thought good to the Holy Ghost and the Fathers assembled in the said general council to make all privy contracts void and of no strength, except the contract be made in the presence of the priest and other witnesses: so that after the publication of the said general council, all such privy contracts without the witness of the priest and others be void and of no effect, but that the parties so privily contracting may lawfully marry any other.

If any man and woman speak the formal words of Matrimony for fear of their parents or friends, or for any evil purpose without consent of heart, they be not man and wife before God. If either of them do use carnal copulation with other that gave no consent in heart, they commit fornication as long as he or she continue in the same mind; wherein the next remedy is to give consent of heart to that which was spoken before in words, and so be they man and wife before God.

166. How many things be required in Matrimony of necessity?

TWO things: consent of both their hearts and words, expressing the consent of both their minds. Also some things be required in Matrimony, that the ordinary for some necessary causes may dispense in: As that banns ought to be asked three solemn days before the time of marriage as the Ordinal doth plainly appoint. And certain time and days in the year, the ordinance of holy Church doth forbid marriage to be solemnized; that they may give themselves more conveniently to prayer, as the Scripture doth teach.

The times that the solemnization of Matrimony doth cease in the Catholic Church[108] is from the Saturday next before Advent Sunday, until the Octave of the Epiphany; from the Saturday next before Septuagesima Sunday, until the Octaves of Easter be past; that is to say, until the Monday next after Low Sunday, from the Sunday before the Rogation week, until Trinity Sunday.

167. How many things do prevent Matrimony from being contracted, and dissolve matrimony that is made?

FIRST, error of the person, when one is brought in for another (except after that it is known, both the parties consent to the marriage). Secondly, when the man is within Holy Orders, or if either of them be professed in Religion or have vowed Chastity. Thirdly, by consanguinity which extendeth to the fourth degree. Fourthly, by affinity which extendeth to the fourth degree. Fifthly, by spiritual kindred, which is between the party that is baptized or confirmed and his Godfathers and Godmothers; and also between the Godfather or Godmother and the parents of the child so baptized or confirmed.

---

[108] 1 Cor 7

Chapter 5

Sobriè, piè and justè vivamus.
Soberly, Godly, and justly let us live.
(Tit 2)

168. How many offices of Christian justice be there?
TWO: the one is to decline from evil, the other is to do good.[109]

169. How can a man be able to perform these two offices of justice?
HE cannot truly of himself; but being helped by the grace of God and instructed by the Holy Ghost, a Christian man may and ought (as much as the state of this life doth permit) to live justly and fulfill the law.[110]

170. By what degrees be we brought into sin?
BY suggestion of the Devil, delectation of the flesh, and consent of the mind.[111]

171. Who be the most grievous sinners?
THEY that sin willfully of mere malice. Also they that do boast of their sin. Thirdly, they that with contentious words strive against them that give them good counsel, and utterly contemn the same.[112]

172. Which be the sins so abominable that cry unto God in heaven for vengeance?
THE Scripture doth make mention of four sins that be most horrible and abominable in the sight of God:

The **first** is voluntary or willful manslaughter. How the innocent blood of Abel cried from the earth to God and how Cain was punished, it is evident.[113]

The **second** is Sodomitical sin: man with man, or woman with woman, against nature. How the cry of this most abominable sin

---
[109] Psa 3; 1 Jn 3; Isa 1
[110] Jn 5; 2 Cor 3; Lk 1; Rom 8; Tit 3
[111] Prov 11; Jn 11
[112] Prov 2
[113] Gen 4

came to God from the earth, and how God poured down fire and brimstone to destroy the wicked Sodomites, it appeareth plain in Scripture.[114] This terrible example putteth in remembrance that perpetually to burn in hell with fire and brimstone is a punishment due for them that commit sin against nature.

The **third** is oppression of the poor, fatherless children, and widows. How God punished Pharaoh and the Egyptians for oppressing the Israelites, the Scripture doth show.[115] Oppressors cannot escape God's vengeance.

The **fourth** sin that crieth to God for vengeance is to keep back the wages of the hired servant or workman when he hath done his service or work.[116]

173. Whether it is not sufficient for a Christian man to do no evil?

TO do no evil is but the half part of Christian justice. It is not sufficient for a Christian man to do no evil, but he is bound to do good.[117] For, as St. James saith, he that knoweth how to do good and doth it not, he doth commit sin.[118] And also the Gospel saith every tree that doth not bring forth good fruit, it shall be cut down and cast into the fire.[119]

174. What kind of good works ought a Christian man to use?

FASTING, almsdeeds, mercy, and prayer. That prayer is good (saith the Scripture) that is joined with fasting and almsdeeds.[120]

175. What is Fasting?

FASTING is a foundation of virtue whereby vice and sin is repressed and the mind is lifted up; the body is chastised, and the flesh is made subject to the spirit; obedience is exercised, and the grace of God obtained. By fasting the soul is nourished.[121]

The manner of fasting is: certain days and times according to the custom and precept of the Church, to abstain from flesh and to eat

---

[114] Gen 18
[115] Ex 22
[116] Jas 5
[117] Psa 36; Rom 12
[118] Jas 4
[119] Mt 3
[120] Tob 21
[121] Hieronymus

but one moderate meal in the day.[122] The time of the Lent is more straightly to be kept than other times of fasting, because Lent hath for it the institution of Christ. The sixth general council in the Lent time doth forbid to eat eggs or cheese, except as necessity require or dispensation be obtained.[123]

176. What is prayer?

PRAYER is a lifting up of the mind to God, whereby we desire evil or adversity to be put away, or else we desire good things to ourselves or to others, or we do praise God.[124]

177. What is almsdeeds or mercy?

IT is a benefit wherewith we help and succor the necessity or misery of others for the honor of God, with a good affection and compassion.

178. How many kinds of alms or mercies be there?

THERE be two kinds of alms or works of mercy: the one is called corporal, the other spiritual.[125]

The **works of mercy or pity corporal** be seven: To feed the hungry, to give drink to the thirsty, to clothe the naked, to visit the prisoners and sick, to harbor the harborless, and bury the dead.

The **works of mercy or pity spiritual** be seven: Discretely to correct them that offend, to teach the ignorant, to give good counsel to them that have need, to pray unto God for the health of our neighbor, to comfort the comfortless, patiently to suffer injuries, to forgive offenses done against us.[126] God grant us to do, that we may live.

AND here now let us make an end. For after thou knowest once, Gentle Reader or diligent learner, what thou ought to believe and how thou oughtest to live (which two points I have prosecuted in this short Catechism), what remaineth but to make an end? For the rest now is to be committed unto thy practice: that like as thou knowest through my simple and plain instruction what is to be done, so study

---

[122] Concil. Magüt. c. 35. &. Bracca. 8. capi. 9.
[123] Council of Constantinople III
[124] Damas.
[125] Mt 25
[126] 1 Thess 5; Jas 5; Tom 15; Mt 6, 28

thou and labor to exemplify and show in thy conversation that which thou knowest. Especially whereas I now have no more to say unto thee, and God will begin to have a saying unto thee, except thou keepest his laws and Commandments. For when the Son of Man shall come in his Majesty and all his Angels with him, then shall he sit upon the seat of his Majesty and all nations shall be gathered together before him, etc.[127] The wicked shall go into everlasting punishment, and the just into life everlasting.

Be faithful therefore in all articles that are to be believed, be devout in thy prayers, be loving and obedient as touching the Commandments of God and his Church, be wise in receiving the Sacraments, and make not light of the remedies of thy sins and infirmities. Be diligent in the works of mercy, and take in good part this my small labor, which, I trust, shall bring great profit unto thee; and God grant it may be so great, as I have and shall wish it to be. Amen.

---

[127] Mt 15

SECTION II
Concerning Ceremonies

Chapter 6

MANY wise and learned men have thought it good that I should join to the Catechism (which I did lately set forth for the instruction of young children in matters of the Faith) a brief declaration of certain Ceremonies whose signification is not so well known to the ignorant people as they should be.

It is therefore first to be known that no company of men can meet together in one mind and consent of heart for the true service of God, except they have certain holy signs; whereby both their worship towards God may be stirred up, and the profession thereof towards their neighbors may be seen.[128] And thereupon as well in the law of the Jews as of the Christians, holy signs and Ceremonies have been always in use, by the appointment of God himself or of his Prophets and Apostles. But for so much as the state of the Jews did bear outwardly a form and show of serving God rather like children than like men, yea rather in a bound than in a free sort, their Ceremonies were in a manner all expressly named in the Law like unto them; because it was presupposed that they of themselves were not able to judge what was convenient for this or that Sacrifice, or else for this or for that time, unless it were by their master and Lawmaker namely prescribed and appointed.

But for so much as the state of the New Testament is free, as wherein men of all nations are taught of God himself and are anointed inwardly with the Holy Ghost, having the law, not of Moses, but of God written in their hearts and bowels (as the Prophets and Apostles do witness), therefore (the holy Sacraments being *made and instituted of Christ himself*) most of the other ceremonies were left to the discretion of the Apostles and their successors.[129] For which cause St. Peter with the rest of the Apostles and Priests at Jerusalem ordained and decreed what was to be observed of the Gentiles, who were newly converted to the Faith. And St. Paul having declared what he received of Christ touching the Sacrament of the Altar, addeth of his own authority: *Caetera cum venero. Disponam* - The rest I will set in order, when I shall come.[130]

---

[128] Augustine, *Contra Faustum* Bk. 19, Ch. 11
[129] Isa 54; Jn 6; 1 Jn 2; Jer 31; Heb 8, 10; 2 Cor 3
[130] 1 Cor 11:23, 34

Upon which words of St. Paul, the great Clerk St. Augustine writeth thus: *Apostolus de hoc Sacramento loquens, ait: Caetera cum venero, ordinabo. Vnde intelligi datur, quia multum erat, vt in epistola totu illum agendi ordinem insinuaret. quem unviuersa per orbem seruat Ecclesia, ab ipso ordinatum esse, quod nulla morum diuersitate variatur.*[131] "The Apostle speaking of this sacrament, saith: 'The rest I will set in order, when I shall come.' Whereupon it is given us to understand, because it was much or hard to touch in an epistle the whole order in doing that which the whole Church throughout the whole world doth observe, that thing which is varied with no diversity of customs to have been ordained by the Apostle Saint Paul." Mark what St. Augustine saith, wherein so ever all churches agree in celebrating Mass; that thing he doubteth not to have been ordained of St. Paul.

Of this kind are holy Altars, secret praying at certain times of the Mass, praying for the living and for the faithful souls departed, the use of receiving the Blessed Sacrament in the morning, or fasting, with many other like ceremonies; which all churches in all countries have always used. And that which is namely said of the ceremonies belonging to the chief Sacrament is likewise to be understood of all other Sacraments. For the Apostle said generally: *State et tenete traditions, quas didicitis siue per sermone, siue per epistola nostra;* Stand steady, and keep ye the traditions which ye have learned either by our talk, or by our letters.[132] And St. Augustine says likewise generally: *Quoe no scripta, sed tradita custodimus, etc.*[133] Those things which we keep, not being written, but being delivered, which at the least are observed throughout the whole world, and are understood to be kept by the commending and decreeing of the Apostles themselves, or else of the general Councils whose authority is most wholesome in the Church. As that the Passion of our Lord, and Resurrection, and Ascension into heaven, and the coming from heaven of the Holy Ghost are solely kept every year; and so of any other thing which is kept in every place where the Church spreads itself.

It were easy to show that many other ancient Fathers do speak in like sort of our holy Ceremonies, were it not above the measure of a brief Catechism to stand about that matter any longer. Therefore now I will talk more particularly of certain special Ceremonies, and the meaning thereof.

---

[131] Augustine, *Letter 54*
[132] 2 Thess 2
[133] Augustine, *Letter 54*

179. Why is holy water used in the Church?

IT is used to put men in mind of the water of Baptism, wherein their sins were cleansed through the Name of the Blessed Trinity called upon them, and through their own or the Church's faith.[134] And therefore as men by the water of Baptism entered into the Church, which is the mystical body of Christ; so at the entering into the material church, they sprinkled themselves with holy water. For albeit the Baptism itself cannot be repeated, yet the remembrance thereof is most laudably preserved in all good Christians.

180. How old is the use of Holy Water?

IT came even from the Apostles, as it may be thought. For mention thereof is made in the Epistle of Pope Alexander, who was the fifth Bishop of Rome after Saint Peter.

181. Can holy water drive away devils?

NOT only holy water, but many other holy things are of power to drive away devils from their bodies or places who use them in a right faith. For, as through our sins the Devil hath power to use not only his own malice but also God's creatures to our hurt; even so faithful men take power of Christ not only to resist the Devil by their own faith, but also by the creatures *which are sanctified by God's word and prayer.*[135] And so does Theodoretus, an ancient writer of the Ecclesiastical history, witness that devils were cast out in the old time.[136] For whereas the Devil stayed the fire that could have no strength in burning of an idol's temple, Marcellus the Bishop of Apamea caused his Deacon Equitius to bring water in a vessel; which being set under the holy Altar, the Bishop prayed, and when he had made the sign of the Cross upon the water, he willed his faithful Deacon to sprinkle the said water upon the flame, *quo facto contactus aquoe impatien doemon aufegit*; Which being done, the Devil not being able to abide that the water should touch him, fled away.

And verily whosoever nowadays cannot abide to have holy water sprinkled upon him, he may well suspect that a Devil hath power on him, who is afraid of the said holy water and therefore keepeth his servant from it as far as he can. Thus we see both the profit and the antiquity of holy water.

---

[134] Tit 3; Mt 28
[135] 1 Tim 4
[136] Theodoret of Cyrus, *Ecclesiastical History*, Bk. 5, Ch. 21

182. Why is sensing used?

IT betokeneth that as the sweet perfume of frankincense ascendeth up into the air, so our prayers ought to be directed as a sweet smell in the sight of God. And as the Angel taught Tobias to drive away the Devil by kindling of the liver of the fish, even so the like kindling of frankincense with the like faith and devotion doth help to drive away the Devil, and to defend the faithful people from his injuries and assaults.[137]

183. How long hath sensing been used?

EVEN from the Apostles' time as it may appear by the words of Dionysius the Areopagite in his book of the holy order and government of the Church, where he expressly nameth that ceremony.[138] In the solemn Mass also of St. James and Chrysostom it was used.

184. What meaneth Procession?

PROCESSIONS were ordained partly to protest and to show everywhere by our deeds the Christian Faith (as by carrying openly before us the banners and tokens of Christ's death), partly also to betoken that even as we go out of the Church and after a pilgrimage come into it again, so Christ, coming from the bosom of his Father to take flesh of the Blessed Virgin Mary, did after his peregrination made in this world return to his Father again; whither also we hope to follow him.[139]

185. Why is the Cross carried before us in Procession?

TO make us understand that all our pilgrimage in this life ought to be in faith, merit, and example of Christ's painful conversation; by whose only death we come to life if yet we suffer with him, to the end that we may reign and triumph with him.[140]

186. What may we learn by holy candles?

FIRST, that God is a consuming fire; whereof the very burning candle doth warn us.[141] Secondly, that as the candle being one kind of creature consisteth of fire, wax, and wick, so Christ consisteth of the

---

[137] Psa 146; Tobit 6
[138] Pseudo-Dionysius, *Ecclesiastical Hierarchy*, Ch. 3
[139] Psa 18
[140] 1 Pet 2; Phil 2; Rom 3
[141] Deut 4

Godhead, soul, and flesh, all being in one Person. Therefore on Candlemas day, by carrying a holy candle, we do well represent our Lady carrying Christ to the Temple in her arms.[142] Thirdly, we ought always to have the fire of charity in our hearts, as the wise Virgins had.[143] Last of all, by the torches which are lighted at the singing of the Gospel, it is signified that the word of God is the light of our soul.[144]

187. Why are candles set before Images?

TO betoken that their works did so shine before men, that men glorified God in heaven thereby. And Christ himself called St. John the Baptist a burning candle which gave light. And he said to his Apostles: "Ye are the light of the world."[145]

188. What do holy ashes mean?

THEY warn us to do penance as the Ninivites did, and therefore at the beginning of Lent (which is the time of penance) they are laid on our heads or foreheads, to betoken that we must lament our former evil life, according as Christ said: "Except ye do penance, ye shall all perish."[146]

189. Why was the fast of Lent ordained?

TO the intent that we the members should, according to our ability, follow the example of Christ our head; protesting by our deed that he fasted forty days for our necessities, and not for his own. Item as not only Moses but Elias fasted forty days, so was it signified that not only the bond of the law, but also the free grace of the Prophets needed the said fast of forty days; and we are now in a prophetical state, seeing it is written of our time that God will pour his spirit upon every flesh (or nation) and that all men shall be taught of God, as in the old time the Prophets were.[147]

190. Who instituted the fast of Lent?

THE Apostles themselves, as St. Jerome teacheth; and therefore even Ignatius, who was the disciple of the Apostles, commandeth

---

[142] Lk 2
[143] Mt 25
[144] Jerome, *Against Vigilantius*, n. 7
[145] Jn 5
[146] Mt 5; Jn 3; Lk 13
[147] Mt 4; Ex 34; Rev 29; Joel 2; Jn 6

the Christians not to despise the Lent or the forty days, because it containeth a following of Christ's conversation.[148]

191. How is Lent to be fasted?

WITH eating dry meats such as do engender least blood, and consequently do least provoke carnal lusts. For which cause all flesh and white meats are forbidden unless necessity, reasonable dispensation, or a custom lawfully prescribed does otherwise permit.[149] Also except men by age, great labor, or sickness be excused, they ought to take but one meal on a fasting day, which in the old time was toward night. For as the perfect fasting is to eat nothing at all, so in them who cannot bear such an abstinence it is permitted to make one meal. As for drinkings at night, or eating any other thing (which yet may not be a meal) so that no fraud be used; it is sufficient to keep the custom which is allowed by the lawful Bishop of the Church wherein we live.[150]

192. Why are Images covered in the Lent?

AS holy Images are set up in God's church at other times to represent unto us that the Saints reign with God in heaven; so in the Lent they are covered and kept from our sight, to betoken that sins and iniquities (for which we then do penance) divide between God and us, hiding his face and glory from us even as the veil hid Moses' face from the hard-hearted Jews.[151] And therefore when the good Christian looketh up and seeth not the glorious representation of heavenly joy, which in the church was wont by his eye to come to his mind, he has warning thereby to cry out: Woe to me, my sins have hidden God's glory from me, except by his grace I may come to true repentance, and to do penance for them.[152] And so he is warned to call unto God for true contrition, sacramental confession, and temporal satisfaction.

193. What signifieth the veil, which is drawn between the people and the high Altar in the Lent?

AS our first parents having sinned, were kept from Paradise with the fiery sword of the Angel; and as in the tabernacle of Moses there was a veil between the inmost and the outward holy place; and as

---

[148] Jerome, *Letter 41 to Marcellus*; St. Ignatius of Antioch, *Epistle to the Philippians*
[149] Theodoret of Cyrus, *Ecclesiastical History*, Bk 1, Ch. 19
[150] Augustine, *Letter 36*
[151] Isa 54; Ex 34; 2 Cor 3
[152] Isa 59; 1 Cor 7; Jn 20

the letter of the Law is a veil, which keepeth the meaning of the Holy Ghost from them who believe not rightly in Christ; so to us that believe and live not well, our sins are a veil and cover which keep us from Christ.[153] But as by the death of Christ the veil of the temple was torn in sunder and all the secrets of the inmost holy place lay open to them who did believe (in token whereof the Lenten veil is also cast down in the Passion Week); so to them who, after due penance, do again work the will of God through his grace, the veil of iniquity is torn down and the grace of Charity lieth open.[154]

194. Why do the people bear palms the Sunday before Easter?

IN remembrance of the notable, miraculous, and triumphant entry which Christ made into Jerusalem that day; at which time the Israelites did cast not only boughs of trees, but also their garments in his way for honor's sake. And the Children cried: Osanna to the Son of David.[155] All which ceremonies we still maintain to the honor of Christ, as the faithful Israelites once did then; and the Protestants still disdain the same, as once the stubborn and hard-hearted Jews did. Our palm boughs also betoken that we ought to fight against the Devil, the flesh, and the world even until death, as Christ did; in which death both his victory was and ours must be perfectly ended.[156]

195. What signifieth the four and twenty candles that are set up on Wednesday before Easter Eve?

THEY signify the twelve prophets and twelve Apostles, and thereby all just men who by preaching and good life gave unto us light and a true testimony of Christ's Godhead and manhood; but yet they were all after a certain sort dimmed, and (as it were) their light was put out one after another, because they sinned as men, at the least venially. And none of them was that Light which, showing itself without blemish, lighteneth every man coming into this world, which is Jesus Christ the Everlasting Light. And yet for so much as they believed in him, their light in him is now also everlasting.[157]

196. Why is the old fire quenched, and new fire hallowed on Easter Eve?

---

[153] Gen 3; Heb 9; 2 Cor 3
[154] Mt 27
[155] Mk 11
[156] Phil 2; 2 Tim 4
[157] 2 Jn 1; Jn 1; Rev 21

TO show that in Christ we are made new men in spirit, and that we must cast off the old man which came by our parents' carnal generation and take new light of Christ's death and resurrection, walking as the Children of light.[158] Therefore the clergy going to hallow the new fire, saith the Psalm: *Dominus illuminatio mea and salus mea*, The Lord is my light and my Salvation.[159]

197. Why is the Paschal of wax hallowed and set up in the Church?

TO represent Christ, who is the Truth signified by the pillar of fire which gave light to the Children of Israel by night.[160] And as Christ at certain times appeared to his Disciples after his resurrection, so is the Paschal taper in remembrance thereof lighted at certain times from Easter until Ascension.[161]

198. Why is the font hallowed?

BECAUSE the Apostles did so institute, as may appear in St. Dionysius, who lived in their time.[162] Also St. Basil confessed that the custom to bless the water of Baptism came from an unwritten tradition.[163] The feasts of Easter and Whitsunday are chosen for the purpose because in the one, Christ after death rose out of his grave; in the other, he sent down the Holy Ghost. Now in Baptism (as St. Paul saith), we are buried with Christ and rise again to walk with him in a new life, and the sanctification of the new man, which we take and bear, is wrought in Baptism first of all by the Holy Ghost.[164]

199. Why are bells hallowed?

TO the end that nothing may be profane which serveth for God's religion; because he is infinitely holy, whom we serve.[165] And thereby the devils also are the more vexed and driven the farther off, because they know them to be the signs and as it were the trumpets, calling the faithful soldiers to hear God's word and to make common prayer.

---

[158] Eph 4, 5
[159] Psa 26 (27)
[160] Ex 13
[161] Mk 16; Jn 20, 21
[162] Pseudo-Dionysius, *Ecclesiastical Hierarchy*, Ch. 2
[163] Basil, *On the Holy Spirit*, Ch. 27
[164] 1 Cor 15; Acts 2; Rom 6; Eph 4; Tit 3
[165] 1 Pet 1

200. Why is the Church hallowed?

BECAUSE it beareth a figure of the living members of Christ, which is holy and unspotted in her faith and religion.[166] Item to cause the men who come thither to be the more stirred to prayer and to be the sooner heard in a holy place, as it may well appear that the Holy Ghost taught us to believe by the dedication of Solomon's temple; where a special grace is desired for them who pray in the temple dedicated to God's holy name.[167]

201. Why is the Altar consecrated?

THAT the chief protestation and showing of external religion (which is external sacrifice) may be offered upon a most solemn and reverend place. For although the whole Church be generally hallowed, yet the Altar being within the same Church hath a most special sanctification, as which beareth that room in our holy doings which the Cross itself bore, when Christ died upon it. And seeing Noah built an Altar;[168] and Abraham is noted not only to have offered up his son but also to have done it upon the Altar;[169] seeing also that in the tabernacle of Moses and the temple of Solomon, the Altar was so holy that (as our Savior himself saith[170]) it sanctified and made holy the gift which was laid upon it; by the same reason our Altars should much more be hallowed, as which contain that Body upon them for whose sake all Altars were hallowed and all Sacrifices were made. Wherefore Optatus, an ancient writer speaking against the Donatists who in his time destroyed the holy Altars of the Catholics, saith: *Quid est enim Altare, nisi sedes corporis et sanguinis Christi?* For what is the Altar, but the seat of the Body and Blood of Christ?[171] That is to say, the place where Christ's Body and Blood doth remain, during the time of the unbloody Sacrifice.

202. What do the Altar clothes signify?

VERILY they represent the good affection which faithful people have to honor the place of Christ's residence. For as the Apostles, being commanded to bring the ass unto Christ did upon their own good affection cast their clothes upon the ass[172] to the end that Christ's

---

[166] 1 Pet 2
[167] Eph 5; 1 Kings 8
[168] Gen 3
[169] Gen 22; Jas 2
[170] Mt 23
[171] Optatus of Milevis, *Against the Donatists*, Bk. 6
[172] Mt 21

seat might be made the more honorable; so do the faithful followers of the Apostles deck and setteth forth the place where Christ in a mystery presenteth himself unto us. And therefore St. Jerome praises Nepotianus for providing carefully that the Altar might be neat and clean: *Erat solicitus si niteret altare, si parietes absque fuliqine, si pauimenta tersa, si ianitor creber in porta, vela semper in ostiis, si sacrificium mundum, si vasa luculenta, and in omnes ceremonias pia solicitudo disposita;*[173] He was careful to see that the Altar might shine, that the walls might be without the smoke and the tapers or lamps, that the pavements might be neat, that the porter might be often at the Church door, that the clothes might always cover the doors, that the Vestry might be clean, that the vessels might be bright, and that his godly carefulness might be well disposed toward all the Ceremonies.

203. What meaneth the apparel which the Priest weareth at Mass?

THE **Amice**, which the Priest first putteth on his head, doth signify the cloth wherewith Christ's face was covered whilst the Jews buffeted him, saying: "Prophecy, who did strike thee?"[174] The **Alb**, which is a long white garment, representeth the white coat wherewith Herod did send Christ back to Pilate, reputing him as a fool.[175] The **Girdle** betokeneth the scourge wherewith Christ was whipped.[176] And the **Favell**, which the Priest putteth on his left arm, betokeneth the cord wherewith they bound Christ when they first took him.[177] As also the **Stole** representeth the other ropes wherewith they bound him to the Pillar while they whipped him. The **upper vestment** doth betoken the purple garment wherewith Christ was clothed in derision, when they saluted him king of the Jews.[178] Thus the priest, going to make the sacrifice of the Church which it learned of Christ, doth in outward signs set before our eyes the history of Christ's Passion, which is the true pattern of all sacrifices.[179]

---

[173] St. Jerome, *Letter 60*, "Epitaph for Nepotianus"
[174] Mt 26
[175] Lk 23
[176] Jn 19
[177] Jn 18
[178] Jn 19
[179] Cyprian, *Letter 62*

Chapter 7

THE Priest then being so clothed setteth briefly before us all the life of Christ, but most especially of all the circumstances of his death. He cometh therefore from the vestry to the Altar, as it were showing how Christ came from heaven into this world. He beginneth the Mass with some part of a Psalm, which he repeats twice or thrice, in showing the Prophets and Patriarchs to have prayed for and to have rejoiced at the day of Christ's Incarnation, which they saw in spirit. He crieth out for mercy nine times, giving us to understand, that his Sacrifice dependeth upon Christ, and not upon our merits.[180] He beginneth the *Gloria in excelsis Deo*, Glory in the highest unto God; putting us in mind of the hymn and praise which the Angels sang at Christ's birth. And therewith he saith, *The Lord be with you*, which is no more but the prophetical naming of Christ who is called Emanuel, that is to say, the Lord with us.

The Collect signifieth the whole Church with one accord to have prayed for the coming of our Savior, and by him only to trust for salvation. The Epistle doth resemble the preaching of St. John the Baptist. The mourning song of the Graile showeth that penance which ensued among the good men upon St. John the Baptist's preaching.[181] The joyful song Alleluia betokeneth the spiritual joy which, after their penance done, they obtained partly in this life and especially in the life to come; for those who mourn in God shall be comforted.[182] The Gospel betokeneth the preaching of Christ. The Creed witnesseth what great fruit of professing the true Faith ensued upon Christ's preaching, which is not only showed by words but also by works; while the devout persons offer unto God before the Altar some of their temporal goods and substance, either to be consecrated unto God (as bread and wine) or to be distributed to the poor, or else to be employed to the use of the Church, as wax and oil.

At length the Catechumens and learners of the Faith being removed out of the Church, the Christian's proper Sacrifice is begun: at which neither novices in faith nor infidels may be present, because it

---

[180] Jn 8
[181] Mt 3
[182] Mt 5

is most subject to the derision of the wicked.[183] Bread and wine then is brought to the Priest at the Altar, to the end he may do with them as Christ in his last supper did, when he was now going to his death. The Chalice betokeneth the grave; the white corporace betokeneth the white sheet wherein Joseph did fold Christ's body when it was laid into the grave; and the paten representeth the stone wherewith the grave was covered. But because all this is done only to bring Christ's death unto our remembrance, and not to bury Christ again, therefore the priest after the Secret prayer (which Christ also used in the garden before his Passion[184]) crieth: "Lift up your hearts," and again: "Thanks unto our Lord God, who hath both redeemed us and left us these mysteries of his glorious death, resurrection, and ascension." After which praises and thanksgiving by the Priest, all the people, or such as supply their place, do sing in the honor of the Blessed Trinity three times: "Holy, Holy, Holy, the Lord God of hosts, blessed is he that cometh in the name of the Lord, Osanna in the highest."

The Priest now entering into the most holy meditations of Christ's death, commendeth to God the whole Church dispersed throughout the whole world, and those by name for whom he is bound to pray; as the Pope, the Bishop, the King, and his own friends.[185] And because this is the common Sacrifice of all the Church, he reverently maketh mention of the blessed Saints which reign with Christ, and desireth to be helped by their prayers whom he doubteth not to hear him, because they live with Christ and in him see our necessities when we call to them, much better than the Prophets saw the hearts of those who came unto them for aid or succor.[186] And being thus provided, he making many times the sign of the Holy Cross to betoken that all the virtue and power he hath is taken by Christ's death and Passion, cometh at last to take Christ's Person upon him, saying in his name and power over the bread: "This is my Body" and over the wine: "This is my Blood, etc."[187] by which words no faithful man doubteth but that Christ's Body and Blood are made really present under the form of bread and wine. In token of which belief the priest lifteth up the Holy Sacrament, to put us in remembrance how Christ was exalted upon the Cross for us; and the people adore with godly honor the selfsame Body and Blood which died and was shed for us.

---

[183] Pseudo-Dionysius, *Ecclesiastical Hierarchy*, Ch. 3
[184] Mt 26
[185] 1 Tim 2
[186] Phil 1; 1 Kings 3, 10
[187] Mt 26

And then in words also the Priest beseecheth, the said Body and Blood of Christ being most acceptable to God in his own nature, to be accepted also of God in respect of the Church; which, being yet sinful, adventureth to handle and to offer such precious gifts. And then the faithful souls are commended also unto God, to the end that no members of the Church may be omitted of the Church in the common Sacrifice which toucheth the whole body of the Church.

And all this holy secret action is ended with the open pronouncing of our Lord's prayer, by the seven petitions whereof we may call to mind the seven words or sayings which our Lord pronounced alone upon the Cross, over and besides these secret prayers wherein he commendeth to his Father all the Patriarchs, Prophets, just men, and all that ever shall be saved, whether they were then born or no; for signification of the which diverse states in the Church, for all whom Christ's body was broken and vexed upon the cross, the Blessed Sacrament of the Altar is broken into three parts; and the kiss of peace being sent to the faithful that are present (whilst they call for mercy and peace at the hands of the Lamb of God), the whole Sacrifice is received either by the priest alone, if none other be prepared thereunto (as Christ upon the Cross ended his own Sacrifice alone), or if others be ready, they receive also with the priest even as Christ at his supper gave his Sacrament to others also. For as St. Cyprian saith, speaking of this Sacrament, *Passio est Domini sacrificium quod offerimus;* The sacrifice which we offer, is the Passion of our Lord.[188] That is to say, the substance which we offer is the same which suffered and rose again from death.

And therefore, although Christ made the Sacrifice of his supper at the evening to declare that as well the old sacraments as the world itself were now come to their later end; yet we offer in the morning, to show that we take hold of Christ's resurrection also, and live now in a new state of grace. And indeed the very receiving and consuming of the Sacrament by the faithful is a resemblance also of Christ's Ascension, wherein he was taken from our sight into the heavens, whence he sent the Holy Ghost, even as the Priest (having now ended the mysteries with the Collect of thanksgiving) blesseth the people, and departeth into the vestry whence he first came forth.

Thus are the Obsecrations, the Orations, the Postulations and the giving of thanks made, whereof St. Paul wrote unto Timothy.[189] And that according to the mind of St. Augustine, who therein treating

---

[188] Cyprian, *Epistle 62*
[189] 1 Tim 2

upon the word Oratio (which in Greek signified Votum, a vow) doubteth not to say: *Voventer Omnia, quoe offerentur Deo, maxime Sancti Altaris Obatio*; All things are vowed which are offered unto God, especially the Oblation of the holy Altar,[190] where he nameth the Sacrament of Christ's supper the Oblation of the Altar, and expressly teacheth it to be offered and vowed unto God. Unto God, I say, and not (as the Protestants teach) either by the people only to the Priest, or by the Priest only to the people. But he saith: *Sancti Altaris oblatio maxime offertur Deo*; The oblation or offering of the holy Altar, is most of all offered unto God.

This may suffice for a brief instruction of the youth, concerning the most notable and daily Ceremonies of the Church; which who so despiseth, he therein despiseth the whole company of Christians who from the Apostles' time until this hour have used the said Ceremonies at the Service of God; as whereby the mind is provoked to think of God and of the holy Saints much more reverently than otherwise it would. God give every man grace, not to be wise more than he ought, but to be humble and rather to seek what an unknown Ceremony meaneth, than to laugh at that which he knoweth not. For he that by such contempt is ignorant shall not be known of God, as the Apostles threateneth. And he that seeketh as he ought, shall find, as our Savior himself hath said.[191]

---

[190] Augustine, *Epistula 149*
[191] Rom 12; 1 Cor 14; Lk 11

SECTION III

Certain Brief Notes

Chapter 8

Four strong reasons why a man ought to forsake all new doctrines and constantly to cleave to the ancient Religion and doctrine, universally and openly professed in England by all the ancient Kings and people of this Island, ever since the first receiving of the Christian Religion there.

Whereas the Holy Scripture admonisheth us to be constant in faith and not wavering, or yet light in belief: These reasons following inform us that we cannot observe this said admonition if we forsake the said ancient Religion and doctrine, and lean to any other.[192]

FIRST, the said ancient Religion and doctrine is an approved and surely grounded religion and doctrine: for it is the very same which the first preachers of Christian Faith in England did there plant; and the very same which the most ancient Fathers of virtuous life and excellent learning, from age to age in all Christian regions from Christ until this day have held and followed; and therefore by a good consequence it is the Religion and doctrine of the Catholic Church, which all the people are bound to follow.[193] And on the other side, most part of the new doctrines are of a late foundation - devised, set up, and advanced in these later days, and therefore in that point are to be held as suspected, and to be taken heed of, as we are admonished.[194] Many of them are old heresies new scoured, and many years before condemned; and therefore they bring sufficient matter to suspect their favorers in all the rest. And they are also so opposite and repugnant to all the said ancient Religion in so many several points; as if all our ancestors had lived ever in misbelief, and as if true Faith had never been published or at least securely defended until this day – which to affirm, were not only to accuse Christ of breach of promise and to deny the providence of the Holy Ghost in governing the Church, but also absurd and against common sense.[195]

SECONDLY, the Authors and beginners of the new doctrines were and are infamous persons and detected of horrible crimes, as well

---

[192] Gal 19; Jn 4; Mt 24
[193] Mt 18; Mt 24; 1 Tim 3-4; 1 Cor 11
[194] 1 Tim 4; 2 Tim 3
[195] Mt 16; Jn 14-16; Lk 11; 2 Tim 3

before as after their publishing of their doctrines.[196] In so much as if the world had been universally in misbelief until their times (as most untruly and absurdly they pretend), yet is it not probable that God would use any such wicked instruments in so great a cause; neither is there any example that ever He did the like, but the contrary. And as for the first preachers of the said ancient Religion in England, what they were in life and conversation all ancient Histories bear witness, and their works and monuments yet remaining do testify; so as this one comparison may suffice for a testimony against the new gospellers, either to condemn them clearly or at least to hold them for suspected.

THIRDLY, the new doctrines being repugnant in themselves and disagreeing in the chief points of Religion, are without rest and unity of spirit; which defect argues their untruth. But this is not to be found in the said ancient Religion and doctrine.[197]

FOURTHLY, the new doctrines do deprave virginity, abstinence, austerity of life, and Christian discipline; and favoreth liberty so much as they give occasion of licentious and dissolute living, and have the marks which the Scripture giveth of the doctrine of Antichrist. So as the wicked conversation of many of the professors and favorers thereof, appeareth evidently to be the mere fruits of their doctrine: a special note to detect all sects and sectaries.[198]

---

[196] See the lives of Calvin, Beza, and Luther; written in their own time by their familiars, and never yet answered.
[197] Rom 12; 2 Cor 1; Heb 4; Eph 4; Phil 2
[198] 2 Pet 2; 1 Jn 2; Jude

Chapter 9

A Ladder of Six Steps To Heaven

Diligent Examination

THE first degree is diligently to search and examine oneself. Every person ought to speak and confer daily with his inward man or soul before he go to bed saying thus:

> "Oh my soul, how much and in what manner have I this day erred and strayed or loitered from a spiritual or celestial life, how much of this day have I spent in true devotion or exercise of virtue, what kind of thing have I done, said, or thought, for or against my soul's health?"

This first rule or degree is found in diverse places of Holy Scripture, as when the prophet said: I have nightly meditated with my heart and used groaning in my spirit.[199] He said also in another place: I have labored sore in my sighings, I will every night wash my bed and sprinkle my couch with tears.[200] And the king Ezechias said: I will bring to thy remembrance, O Lord God, all my years in bitterness and anguish of my soul.[201]

Detestation

THE second degree is detestation. It behooveth that when any person by this diligent examination have found his conscience loaded or charged with sin, then to detest and hate it for the love of God (to whom all sin is contrary and displeasant), and for no other thing.

Purpose of Amendment

THE third degree is full purpose to amend. After sin be detested must follow to intend and endeavor to do good, for to have at the

---

[199] Psa 77
[200] Psa 6
[201] Isa 38

least some beginning of the two parts of Christian Justice, which are to decline from evil and do good (which is at large defined in the chapter of this present book entreating of the Offices of Christian Justice); for he is unhappy, wicked, and void of understanding, that will not (at the least) purpose and determine every day betwixt God and himself to do better in time to come. And this is to present himself to the grace of God, of the which the prophet speaketh: *Quare tristis es anima mea and quare coturbas me, etc.*; Wherefore art thou heavy my soul and wherefore doest thou trouble me - trust in God, for yet will I confess the praises of him.[202] By these praises is to be understood the good life we lead.

Prayer

THE fourth degree is prayer. After having purposed well and virtuously to live, it behooveth to do all by humble, devout, and perseverant prayer, to the end that we may have help and assistance of God. For without him we cannot enter into any step of virtue, and therefore we ought every day humbly to pray unto God, saying:

> "O most sovereign Lord and God which by Thy benign grace exhorts us by Thy Holy Scripture to trust and put our refuge in Thee by prayers, for that Thou art almighty and vigilant, and incline Thy divinity bounty to our feebleness, we being Thy work and poor creatures; Now then for the love of Thee I renounce all worldly vanities and sensuality, and desire to live well and virtuously in keeping Thy Commandments.
>
> Confirm therefore my desire by Thy Holy Spirit and finally give me such virtues as are to me necessary to bring me to Thee, where is all glory, beatitude, and felicity to all the Just. And thou Blessed Virgin Mary and all the Saints of heaven, it is to you to whom I lift up mine eyes, to the end that by your merits and prayers I may obtain that which my merits could never obtain.
>
> O Jesus, fountain of all secretness, pardon me that I have not until this present sufficiently known thy incomprehensible secretness; neither have I forced myself anything to get at the least, any taste thereof making small account to beautify my soul or to relieve her, nor of the union betwixt her and Thy Holy Spirit. O how little have I withdrawn myself to spiritual

---

[202] Psa 42

things and so to prepare my heart to receive Thee and to be Joyful with Thee, and to make a chamber in me in the which Thou hadst long time and often made Thy dwelling.

Alas my most loyal and true Lover, pardon me that I have not always sought and obeyed according to Thy holy will, that I have not esteemed Thy friendship for my sovereign wealth; but the contrary have as the prodigal child long time served swine and have satisfied myself with their meat, that is to say with vain and wicked delights and pleasures of this world.

Beseeching Thee therefore to forgive me for having begun so late to know Thee, and that I have not before this time endeavored myself to run after the secret odor of Thy ointments - that is to say, after Thy virtues and Thy divine grace - I beseech Thee, withdraw not Thy right hand from me, and disdain not to succor him which commeth though something late, but rather awake me and draw me more strongly because I come so late (for the most part of my days are past over); to the end I may in running hastily to Thee, recover the time past which I lost, and that the hour of death overtake me not before I have taken such state of life as always I ought to purpose and pretend: that is to say a perfect union of my soul and Thy Holy Spirit, through pure and true continual love. Amen.

Execution of Works

THE fifth degree is execution of works. In this point we all fail commonly, for we purpose and pray sometimes enough, but we never come to this degree: to work the said purpose which appertaineth to a virtuous life. It behooveth then, that person that tendeth to perfection (when he riseth in the morning) to say in his heart: "I see and consider well that it behooveth me to use such and such virtue, and therefore this day without any longer delay, I will put in execution the same work," and then he ought effectually and constantly to begin.

Perseverance in Virtue

THE sixth degree is perseverance in virtue. It is necessary also to ascend up to this degree (those that will come to a heavenly and godly life) and not to rest and faint in the way. For it may so happen that some, having served God and lived virtuously for the space of 16 or 20 years, after by little and little shall wax weary and negligent, leaving off his virtuous exercises and God also begin to forsake him; for if God abandon or forsake any, the Devil presently taketh possession to devour him, to make him forget his former good life, and to live wickedly in all vice and sin.

Of this speaketh the prophet David, saying: *Deus dereliquu eum, persequemini and comprehendite eum quia non est qui eripiat*, God hath forsaken him, pursue him and apprehend him for there is none that will deliver him.[203] These are the words of the wicked and reproved spirits, destroyers of souls in speaking one to another. Alas, it is marvelously lamentable when it thus happeneth, and therefore we ought most humbly and often pray unto God with the prophet Daniel, saying: *Ne derelinquas me domine deus neus, nequando rapiat, and non sit qui eripiat*, Forsake me not, my Lord and God, depart not from me lest the Devil come to denounce me and none be that can deliver me. God through his grace grant us this request. Amen.

Examination of Conscience

THE first point is to give God thanks for his benefits received, with this or such like prayer:

> Bless our Lord God (O my soul) and all that is within me bless him. Give thanks to God (my soul) for all his benefits given to me, and see thou never forget them. To Thee O Lord be all thanks, glory and honor for ever more. Amen.

THE next point is to desire God's grace for to know your sins, and to expel the same with this or such like prayer:

> O Lord show to me Thy ways and teach me Thy foot-paths. Pour into my heart O Lord the grace of Thy Holy Spirit, and lighten my understanding, that I may thoroughly perceive and see all my sins before my eyes and by Thy gracious aid expel the same from time to time until my life's end, good Lord I beseech Thee.

---

[203] Psa 71

T HE third point is to call your soul to an account for all your sins that day committed (beginning in the morning at your first waking, and so from hour to hour until the time of this meditation) in thought, word, deed and omission: and to this shall help you, if you call to remembrance what matters you have been occupied withal, and with what persons, and how much time you spent therein.

And first, examine your thoughts: With what idle and unfruitful cogitations you passed this time or that time of the day, if your mind hath been upon worldly things more than need were, or in the time of prayer; or if you have been over careful of your estate, lest by loss of this or that friend you should want; or have had any thought to suspect or misjudge wrongfully; or motion to mistrust God's help, by thinking too much of the loss of any friend or worldly thing; or have had any murmuring against God in any way, and how far you waded in any thought, and whether you gave any consent to your remembrance; or if you have felt any fleshly motions or any carnal delectations, and whether they came in your mind so as you passed them without consent or without strife to your remembrance, or no. Or whether you have had mind to revenge wrongs; or if you have had any thoughts of pusillanimity or discouragement in godly exercise, which is a spice of sloth: As when the Devil doth suggest you think any evil of God or exercise of virtue, or of weariness of the world otherwise than for hate of sin or for love to be with God. Or if any thoughts have drawn you from serving of God in prayers, or at Mass, or in saying penance enjoined, or in receiving the Sacrament; or what other vain thought hath troubled you.

And then examine yourself for words: What superfluous talk for recreation's sake have you used; if you have opened any secret faults of others, or have spoken to the reproach of others anything true or false; or justly have provoked others to anger by talk or hasty speech; or by filthy speech have given to others occasion of sin; or have sworn vainly, or have spoken untruths. And ever foresee that you stand in doubt of your own words, though you remember no ill words to have escaped you. And even so for your works: Whether you have done any works of charity with pure intent, without vainglory or hypocrisy. And here think of Pride, Envy, Wrath, Sloth, Covetousness, Gluttony, and Lechery - how you have actually offended in any of them. If you have not loved God so earnestly as you should; if you have desired any man's death, or killed any man in his good fame; if you have left anything undone which you ought to have done according to your ability touching the work of mercy or deeds of

Charity. And ever suspect your doings in everything, though you remember not any evil done that day. And this examination daily done, will make you more ready for your sacramental confession, and help you in many things.

THE fourth point is with a short confession to ask forgiveness to this effect or like:

> I confess to Thee (O God Almighty, Maker of heaven and earth) all my sins, whatsoever they be which I have committed from my infancy to this present time, wittingly or ignorantly, and especially those which this day I have committed in thought, word, or deed against Thy divine will. And I most humbly crave pardon of Thee, for my sins be innumerable. Mercy, Lord, mercy, I most humbly beseech Thee.

THE fifth point is to purpose with God's grace to amend your life, and say *Pater Noster*, *Ave Maria*.

> Kindle in me (O Lord) the fire of Thy Love, and grant me fruitful amendment of my life, I beseech Thee. Amen.

Chapter 10

JESUS Christ our Savior, the Son of God, for the love he did bear to mankind, came down into the world, suffered death upon the Cross, descended into hell, and with victory over hell, damnation, and death he rose again, and in his glorified body ascended to the glory of his Father; The memory of which victory, and our reconciliation to God the Father, with the whole mystery of our Redemption is celebrated of every good Christian, daily by making the **Sign of the Cross**.

In this Faith and belief all good Christians use oftentimes to make the sign of the cross on their foreheads, as a continual renewing of the badge or mark of their Christian profession, impressed in their foreheads by the priest of God at the font of Baptism.

In this Faith and belief the Church of God hath appointed her children the Catholic Christians at the saying of *Deus in adiutorium* and in other parts of divine service to make the sign of the cross, by drawing the hand from the forehead to the breast, and from the left shoulder to the right; which observation was appointed upon grave considerations, for thereby the good Christian is put in mind of diverse things daily and hourly meet to be thought of.

For the drawing down of the hand from the forehead to the breast reneweth the memory of the coming of the Son of God down into the world to save mankind. The removing of the hand to the left shoulder representeth the descending of our Savior into hell for to obtain victory over hell, damnation and death. The drawing of the hand over heart to the right shoulder for to finish up the figure and shape of the cross resembleth unto us the glorious recourse of our Savior Jesus Christ to his Father, for to consummate our redemption and reconciliation after his death upon the Cross.

And for so much as by the left hand in an apt form of speech all sinister and evil things are signified, and good things by the right hand: therefore the good Christian, by drawing off the hand from the left shoulder to the right, is put in mind that he must withdraw his cogitation, care, and study from all worldly vanities and sinister allurements of our ghostly enemies, and to fix his heart and mind on heaven and heavenly things; That he must eschew the broad way of sin which lieth on the left hand, and tread the strait path of virtuous conversation on the right hand; And that by the benefit of the Cross, he is put in hope to pass from temporal to everlasting pleasures and commodities: to avoid eternal misery and obtain sempiternal felicity.

THE

CHRISTIAN DOCTRINE
in manner of a Dialogue be-
tweene the Master and
the Disciple

*Made by the Reuer. Fa. Iames
Ledesma of the Society
of Iesus.*

Now lately translated into
English, for the vse of
children, and other
vnlearned Ca-
tholickes.

1597.

Original Title Page
(London[?]: Secret Press, 1597)

The Christian Doctrine
In Manner of a Dialogue Betweene the Master and the Disciple

Made by the Rever. Fa. James Ledesma
of the Society of Jesus.

Now lately translated into English, for the use
of children, and other unlearned Catholickes.

1597.

Chapter 1

Of the Name and Sign of a Christian

1. Are you a Christian?
YEA, by the grace of our Lord Jesus Christ.

2. What is a Christian?
THE Disciple of Christ: that is, he which having been baptized, believeth and maketh open profession of the law of Christ.

3. What do you understand Christ to be?
HE is true God and true man.

4. Which is the Sign of a Christian?
THE Sign of the Holy Cross, which is made by putting the hand unto the head, and under the breast, and then at the left shoulder, and the right, saying: "In the Name of the Father, and of the Son, and of the Holy Ghost. Amen."

5. Why is it made in this manner?
TO signify unto us two great mysteries: The one of the most Holy Trinity, the other of the Incarnation of our Lord Jesus Christ, who died for us upon the Cross.

Of the End of Man

6. For what end was man created?
FOR to love and serve God in this life; and afterward, for to see him and enjoy him in the other life.

7. How many things are necessary for a Christian that he may attain his end, and be saved?
FOUR: Faith, Hope, Charity, and good works.

8. What do you believe by Faith?
ALL that which the holy Catholic Roman Church believeth and holdeth; and principally, that which is contained in the Creed.

9. Say the Creed.
CREDO *in Deum Patrem omnipotentem, Creatorem coeli et terrae*
Et in Iesum Christum, Filium eius unicum, Dominum nostrum
Qui conceptus est de Spiritu Sancto, natus ex Maria Virgine
Passus sub Pontio Pilato, crucifixus, mortuus, et sepultus
Descendit ad inferos, tertia die resurrexit a mortuis
Ascendit ad coelos, sedet ad dexteram Dei Patris omnipotentis
Inde venturus est iudicare vivos et mortuos.
Credo in Spiritum Sanctum
Sanctam Ecclesiam catholicam, sanctorum communionem
Remissionem peccatorum
Carnis resurrectionem
Vitam aeternam. Amen.

I BELIEVE in God the Father Almighty, maker of heaven and earth.
And in Jesus Christ, his only Son our Lord.
Which was conceived by the Holy Ghost, born of the Virgin Mary.
Suffered under Pontius Pilate, was crucified, dead and buried.
He descended into Hell, the third day he rose again from the dead.
He ascended into Heaven, and sitteth at the right hand of God the Father Almighty.
From thence he shall come to judge the quick and the dead.
I believe in the Holy Ghost.
The holy Catholic Church, the Communion of Saints.
The forgiveness of sins.
The resurrection of the flesh.
And the life everlasting. Amen.

Of the Creed

10. What have we said?
THE Creed.

11. Who made it?
THE Twelve Apostles, when they were to go forth to preach the Gospel through all the world.

12. Wherefore did they make it?
FOR to instruct us in the Faith.

13. What is contained in the Creed?
TWELVE articles: that is, twelve principal parts of our Faith.

Of Some Principal Articles of the Creed

14. In whom do you believe?
I BELIEVE in God.

15. What is God?
HE is the Creator and governor of heaven and earth, and Lord of all things.

16. Why is God said to be almighty?
BECAUSE with his very will only and infinite power he can make and destroy every thing.

17. What do you believe that the most Holy Trinity is?
IT is that very same God: the Father, the Son, and the Holy Ghost; three Persons, and only one God.

18. Is the Father God?
YEA forsooth.

19. Is the Son God?
YEA forsooth.

20. Is the Holy Ghost God?

YEA forsooth.

21. Be there three Gods?

NO forsooth. For although there be three Persons, yet there is but only one God.

22. What similitude can you give me of the most Holy Trinity?

EVEN as we that are made according to His image and likeness have only one soul, and three powers thereof: memory, understanding, and will.

23. Do you believe in Jesus Christ?

YEA forsooth.

24. What do you think Jesus Christ to be?

HE is the Son of God the Father; altogether as mighty, as wise, as good as the Father; which Son of God became man for us in the womb of the glorious Virgin Mary, by the work of the Holy Ghost.

25. What other thing hath Christ done for us?

HE was born of the same Virgin Mary, she remaining a Virgin before her childbirth, in her childbirth, and after her childbirth.

26. And what more?

HE was crucified, died, and was buried, descended into hell, and the third day he rose again from the dead. He ascended into heaven, and sitteth at the right hand of God the Father almighty, as his Son. From thence he shall come to judge the quick and the dead, for to render to everyone according to their works.

27. Do you believe in the Holy Ghost?

YEA forsooth, for he is true God, and the Third Person of the most holy Trinity: who giveth his grace and his gifts to the holy Catholic Church.

28. What is the holy Catholic Church?

IT is the whole congregation of the faithful Christians, who have and confess the faith of Jesus Christ: the head of which Church is Christ himself, and the Pope his Vicar on earth.

29. What good have we in the Church?
THIS: that we are partakers of all the sacrifices, sacraments, and good works which are done therein; and we have the remission of sins, with many other graces and gifts of God.

30. What is the resurrection of the flesh, and the life everlasting?
IT is, that at the day of judgment everyone shall rise again with the very same body and soul; and the good shall go into everlasting life, for to see and enjoy God – and the evil into Hell, with the Devils.

31. Who goeth to the pains of Purgatory?
THE souls of those which die in the grace of God but have not yet fully satisfied for their sins. After that they have suffered the due punishments, they shall go to heaven.

Chapter 2

Of Hope

32. What do you look to have by Hope in God?

THE life everlasting; which principally is obtained by the grace of God, and besides by the merits which, through the same grace, proceed from us.

33. For to obtain that which we hope for, what is required?

AMONGST other things, Prayer.

34. What prayers doth the Church teach us?

THE *Pater Noster*, the *Ave Maria*, the *Salve Regina*, and others.

35. Say the Pater Noster.

PATER Noster, qui es in caelis, sanctificetur nomen tuum. Adveniat regnum tuum. Fiat voluntas tua, sicut in caelo et in terra. Panem nostrum quotidianum da nobis hodie, et dimitte nobis debita nostra sicut et nos dimittimus debitoribus nostris. Et ne nos inducas in tentationem, sed libera nos a malo. Amen.

OUR Father which art in Heaven, hallowed be thy name. Thy kingdom come. Thy will be done in earth, as it is in heaven. Give us this day our daily bread. And forgive us our trespasses, as we forgive them that trespass against us. And lead us not into temptation. But deliver us from evil. Amen.

Of the *Pater Noster*

36. What have we said?

THE *Pater Noster.*

37. Who made it?

OUR Lord Jesus Christ. He spoke it with his most holy mouth and gave it to his Disciples, and therefore it is the most excellent of all prayers.

38. What do we ask in this prayer?

FIRST we ask the glory of God, and then our own good for soul and body, and that he will deliver us from all evil.

39. With whom do we speak therein?

WITH our Lord God.

40. Where is God?

HE is in every place: but he is said principally to be in heaven, where he doth manifest himself unto the Blessed.

Of the *Ave Maria*

AVE Maria, gratia plena, Dominus tecum. Benedicta tu in mulieribus, et benedictus fructus ventris tui, Iesus. Sancta Maria, Mater Dei, ora pro nobis peccatoribus, nunc, et in hora mortis nostrae. Amen.

HAIL Mary, full of grace, our Lord is with thee; blessed art thou among women, and blessed is the fruit of thy womb, Jesus. Holy Mary, Mother of God, pray for us sinners, now, and in the hour of our death. Amen.

41. What have we said?

THE *Ave Maria.*

42. Who made it?

THE Angel Gabriel, when he came to salute our Lady: whereunto are adjoined some words of St. Elizabeth and of the Church.

43. With whom do we speak in the *Ave Maria*?

WITH our Lady.

44. What do you believe our Lady to be?

SHE is Mother of God, a Virgin, full of grace and of all virtue, Queen of heaven and of earth, and our advocate.

45. Where is our Lady?

SHE is in heaven.

46. What say you of her which is in the Church?

THAT is the Image of her which is in heaven, for to put us in mind of her. And because it is her image, we do reverence unto it, in honor of her.

47. As there are many Images of our Lady, be there also many Ladies?

NO forsooth: but one only which is in heaven, whom those Images on earth do represent.

48. Why then is she called, our Lady of Pity, of Remedy, of Consolation, and in other like sort?

FOR the many and diverse benefits which she doth us.

49. What do we say to her in the *Ave Maria*?
WE salute her and praise her, recommending ourselves unto her.

Of the *Salve Regina*

SALVE Regina, mater misericordiae, vita, dulcedo, et spes nostra, salve. Ad te clamamus exsules filii Hevae. Ad te suspiramus, gementes et flentes in hac lacrimarum valle. Eia, ergo, advocata nostra, illos tuos misericordes oculos ad nos converte. Et Iesum, benedictum fructum ventris tui, nobis post hoc exsilium ostende. O clemens, O pia, O dulcis Virgo Maria. Amen. Ora pro nobis, sancta Dei Genetrix, Ut digni efficiamur promissionibus Christi.

50. What have we said?
THE *Salve Regina*.

51. Who taught it to us?
OUR holy mother the Church.

52. To whom do we speak?
WITH the same Virgin Mary.

53. What do we say unto her in it?
OTHER praises of the same Virgin, entreating withal her holy favor and help.

Of Other Prayers and Invocation of Saints

54. After the Virgin Mary, have you devotion to other Saints?
YEA forsooth, unto all – as unto the friends of God and our intercessors in heaven – but especially unto my Angel keeper and the Saint of my name.

55. And unto the Relics of Saints?
I HONOR them also, because they have been the temple of the Holy Ghost and are to be reunited to their glorious souls.

56. What Prayer do you make unto Saints?

THOSE which the Church doth teach us; and also for their honor and that they may pray for me, I say the *Pater Noster* and *Ave Maria*.

57. What do you when you go to bed?

TWO things: First, having made the Sign of the Cross, I examine my conscience. Secondly, I say the general Confession, the *Pater Noster*, and the *Ave Maria*, and my other devotions.

Of the Examining of Our Conscience

58. How do you examine your conscience?

FIRST, I thank God for the benefits received, especially of that day.

59. What more?

WHEN I think of my sins, especially of that day; being sorry for them, with purpose of amending and of confessing them.

60. What then?

FINALLY, I ask God pardon, and make a firm purpose of sinning no more.

61. And what do you in the morning?

THREE things: First, I thank God that he hath kept me that night, and for his other benefits.

62. What is the second thing you do?

I OFFER him my body and soul.

63. What is the third?

I BESEECH him that whatsoever I shall do may be for his holy service, and also I say my other devotions mental and vocal; that is, with the mind and with the voice.

Chapter 3

Of Charity

64. Which is the third thing necessary for a Christian?
CHARITY.

65. Whom ought we to love with charity?
GOD above all things, and our neighbor as ourselves, for the love of God.

66. How shall we love our neighbor as ourselves?
DESIRING for him and doing unto him that which we would for ourselves, according unto reason and the law of God.

Of Good Works

67. Which is the fourth thing necessary for a Christian?
GOOD works. For after one is come to the years of discretion, faith is not sufficient without good works.

68. What good works are these?
THOSE which are ordained in the Ten Commandments of God and in the other Commandments of the Church, with the works of mercy and of other virtues.

69. Say the Ten Commandments.
   1. I am Thy Lord God, thou shalt have no other Gods but me.
   2. Thou shalt not take the name of God in vain.
   3. Remember to sanctify the holy days.
   4. Honor thy father and mother.
   5. Thou shalt not kill.
   6. Thou shalt not commit adultery.
   7. Thou shalt not steal.
   8. Thou shalt not bear false witness.
   9. Thou shalt not desire thy neighbor's wife.
   10. Thou shalt not desire thy neighbor's goods.

Of the Ten Commandments

70. Where did God give these Ten Commandments?
FIRST, in the Old Law; and afterwards, Christ our Lord confirmed them in the New.

71. What is contained in them?
THE first three (of worshipping one God, of not taking his Name in vain, and of sanctifying the holy days) do appertain to the honor of God, because he is to be honored first with the heart, then with the tongue, and then with deeds.

72. And the other seven?
THEY appertain to the profit of our neighbor.

73. These Ten Commandments - in how many are they comprehended?

IN the two precepts of Charity: that is, to love God above all things, and our neighbor as ourselves.

74. So that the whole Law of God is comprehended in this sweet precept of love, which our Lord grant us for his infinite goodness. Amen.

Of the Commandments of the Church

75. Say the Commandments of the Church.
1. To hear Mass on the holy days commanded.
2. To fast during Lent and other days commanded, and to abstain from flesh meat on the accustomed days.
3. To go to Confession at least once a year.
4. To receive Communion at least at Easter.
5. To pay tithes.

Of the Seven Capital Sins

76. We have spoken of the good works which are to be done. Say now the evil which must be shunned: and first, of the seven sins which are called mortal.
1. Pride
2. Covetousness
3. Lechery
4. Anger
5. Gluttony
6. Envy
7. Sloth

These are cause and heads of all other sins, and therefore are called Capital, although sometimes they may be venial.[*]

---

[*] A sinner's personal culpability determines whether a given commission of one such capital sin becomes mortal, i.e., destructive of grace in the soul (see n. 78 below).

77. What is sin?

IT is that which is thought, spoken, or done contrary to the law and will of God.

78. What harm doth mortal sin to the sinner?

IT maketh him lose God and his grace, and the glory which was promised him; and it maketh him inherit the everlasting pain of Hell.

79. Why is it called mortal?

BECAUSE it killeth the soul, making it to lose the life of grace.

80. What doth venial sin?

IT causeth not the loss of God's grace, neither deserveth hell; but it maketh a man to wax cold in the love and service of God and meriteth temporal punishment, and disposeth him also unto mortal sin.

Chapter 4

Of the Seven Sacraments

81. What other thing is necessary for us?

IT is necessary that we know the holy Sacraments, and that we receive them in due time when our holy mother the Church so commandeth and declareth unto us.

82. For what end?

FOR the blotting out of our sins and obtaining of God's grace, and help for the doing of good works.

83. Say the Sacraments of our holy mother the Church.
1. Baptism
2. Confirmation
3. Eucharist
4. Penance
5. Extreme Unction
6. Holy Orders
7. Matrimony

An Exposition of Some Sacraments

84. Who hath ordained these Sacraments?
OUR Lord Jesus Christ.

85. Wherefore?
FOR to give us pardon of our sins and to communicate unto us his grace and the merits of his Passion; and in each one there is given grace for some particular thing, but it is required that we receive them worthily.

86. What effect hath the Sacrament of Baptism?
IT maketh us Christians, and the children of God.

87. How is this brought to pass?
BECAUSE we are all born in Original Sin; which together with all other sins committed before Baptism is taken away by the same; and there is given us God's grace and his other gifts. And so we are made children of God, and heirs of everlasting life.

88. For what effect serveth the Sacrament of Confession or Penance?
THAT God our Lord may pardon our sins which we have done after Baptism.

89. How must he prepare himself, that will be confessed?
HE must do three things: First, he must procure with diligence to call to mind his sins committed. Secondly, to have sorrow and repentance with purpose of sinning no more. Thirdly, he must make a

full confession of them all, and fulfill his penance given him by his Confessor.

90. For what effect serveth the Sacrament of the Altar?

FIRST, that our soul may be nourished and fed with the grace of God and united unto him. Secondly, that we fall not easily into sin. Thirdly, for to obtain all perfection.

91. Who is in the Blessed Sacrament?

JESUS Christ our Lord: in body, soul, and Godhead, even as he is in heaven; as well in the Host as in the Chalice; after the Consecration of the Priest which is made during the Mass.

92. What is the Mass?

IT is a memory and true representation of the life, passion, and death of our Lord Jesus Christ; and it is withal a Sacrifice, where Christ himself is offered for the quick and the dead. And therefore we must be present thereat, with great devotion and attention.

93. How must one prepare himself to receive worthily the Blessed Sacrament?

BY going with devotion, without conscience of mortal sin, and being first confessed.

94. For what effects do the other sacraments serve?

FOR to receive diverse graces of God, for that end for which they were ordained.

Of Other Things

95. Say the other things which belong to good works or to the Christian doctrine; and first, say the Three Theological Virtues.

FAITH, Hope, and Charity.

96. Say the Four Cardinal Virtues.
 1. Prudence.
 2. Fortitude.
 3. Justice.
 4. Temperance.

97. Say the Seven Gifts of the Holy Ghost.
 1. The gift of Wisdom.
 2. of Understanding.
 3. of Counsel.
 4. of Fortitude.
 5. of Knowledge.
 6. of Piety.
 7. And the gift of the Fear of God.

98. Say the Eight Beatitudes.
 1. Blessed are the poor of spirit, for theirs is the kingdom of heaven.
 2. Blessed are the meek, for they shall possess the earth.
 3. Blessed are they that mourn, for they shall be comforted.
 4. Blessed are they that hunger and thirst after Justice, for they shall have their fill.
 5. Blessed are the merciful, for they shall obtain mercy.
 6. Blessed are the clean of heart, for they shall see God.
 7. Blessed are the peacemakers, for they shall be called the children of God.
 8. Blessed are they that suffer persecution for Justice, for theirs is the Kingdom of heaven.

99. Say the Twelve Fruits of the Holy Ghost.
 1. Charity.
 2. Joy.
 3. Peace.
 4. Patience.

5. Longanimity.
   6. Goodness.
   7. Benignity.
   8. Meekness.
   9. Faith.
   10. Modesty.
   11. Continency.
   12. Chastity.

100. Say the Seven Corporal Works of Mercy.
   1. To feed the hungry.
   2. To give drink to the thirsty.
   3. To clothe the naked.
   4. To harbor pilgrims.
   5. To visit the sick.
   6. To visit prisoners.
   7. To bury the dead.

101. Say the Seven Spiritual Works of Mercy.
   1. To give good counsel to others.
   2. To instruct the ignorant.
   3. To admonish those who sin.
   4. To comfort the afflicted and troubled.
   5. To pardon offenses and injuries received.
   6. To bear patiently the troublesomeness of others.
   7. To pray for the quick and the dead.

102. Say the fifteen mysteries of the life of our Lord Jesus Christ, for to meditate and say the Rosary of our Lady. And first, say the five Joyful.
   1. The Annunciation of our Lady when the Son of God was conceived.
   2. The Visitation of Saint Elizabeth.
   3. The Nativity of our Lord Jesus Christ.
   4. The Presentation of our Lord in the Temple.
   5. When our Lord was found again in the Temple amongst the Doctors.

103. Say now the five Sorrowful.
   1. The Prayer of our Lord in the garden.
   2. The Whipping at the pillar.

3. The Crowning with a crown of thorns.
4. The Carrying of the Cross unto Mount Calvary.
5. The Crucifying and Death of the Cross.

104. Say the five Glorious.
1. The Resurrection of our Lord.
2. His Ascension unto heaven.
3. The Coming of the Holy Ghost.
4. The Assumption of our Lady.
5. Her Coronation above all Angels and Saints.

105. When the bell ringeth to the *Ave Maria,* how may we obtain indulgence?

By saying at the first toll: *Angelus Domini nuntiavit Mariae; et concepit de Spiritu Sancto. Ave Maria,* etc.

At the second toll: *Ecce Ancilla Domini; fiat mihi secundum verbum tuum. Ave Maria,* etc.

At the third toll: *Et verbum caro factum est, et habitavit in nobis. Ave Maria,* etc.

And concluding: *Oremus. Gratiam tuam, quaesumus, Domine, mentibus nostris infunde; ut qui, Angelo nuntiante, Christi Filii tui incarnationem cognovimus, per passionem eius et crucem, ad resurrectionis gloriam perducamur. Per eundem Christum Dominum nostrum. Amen.*

A Prayer Before Study

Clementissime Pater, infunde nobis per meritu Iesu Christi filii tui Spiritus Sancti gratiam, qua intellectus noster liberalibus disciplinis plenius illustretur, quas in divinum tuum honorem aliquando, et nostram spiritualem utilitatem convertere possimus. Per Christum Dominum nostrum. Amen.

About This Series

TRADIVOX was first conceived as a research endeavor to recover lost and otherwise little-known Catholic catechetical texts. As the research progressed over several years, the vision began to grow, along with the number of project contributors and a general desire to share these works with a broader audience.

Legally incorporated in 2019, Tradivox, Inc. has begun the work of carefully remastering and republishing dozens of these catechisms which were once in common and official use in the Church around the world. That effort is embodied in this *Tradivox Catholic Catechism Index*, a multi-volume series restoring artifacts of traditional faith and praxis for a contemporary readership. More about this series and the work of Tradivox, Inc. can be learned at www.Tradivox.com.